IMRE VALLYON

THE New Heaven & THE New Earth

Sounding-Light
Publishing

The New Heaven and The New Earth, by Imre Vallyon
First edition, July 2014

ISBN 978-0-909038-68-7

Sounding-Light Publishing
PO Box 771, Hamilton 3240, New Zealand
www.soundinglight.com

CONTENTS

A NOTE ON SANSKRIT USAGE

The Sanskrit language is SAṄSKṚTA, meaning "well-made, perfectly polished". It is also called DEVANĀGARĪ, "God's writing". It is the most ancient sacerdotal (priestly) language of India, used for writing the scriptures, mythologies and sciences of the ancient Indian Subcontinent.

Sanskrit is a multi-layered language. It is a language which has the highest number of esoteric, spiritual and religious words, terms and expressions. There is no other language like it on Earth. The spiritual and esoteric terms run into thousands and thousands.

This work describes the pronunciation of the Sanskrit words by way of transliterated spellings, along with esoteric and spiritual meanings as perceived in Higher Consciousness. A pronunciation guide can be found at the back of the book. Sanskrit words are pluralized using a small 's' (e.g. mantras) to remind the reader that this English convention is not part of the original language. The purpose of this device is to preserve the sound-structures of the Sanskrit words.

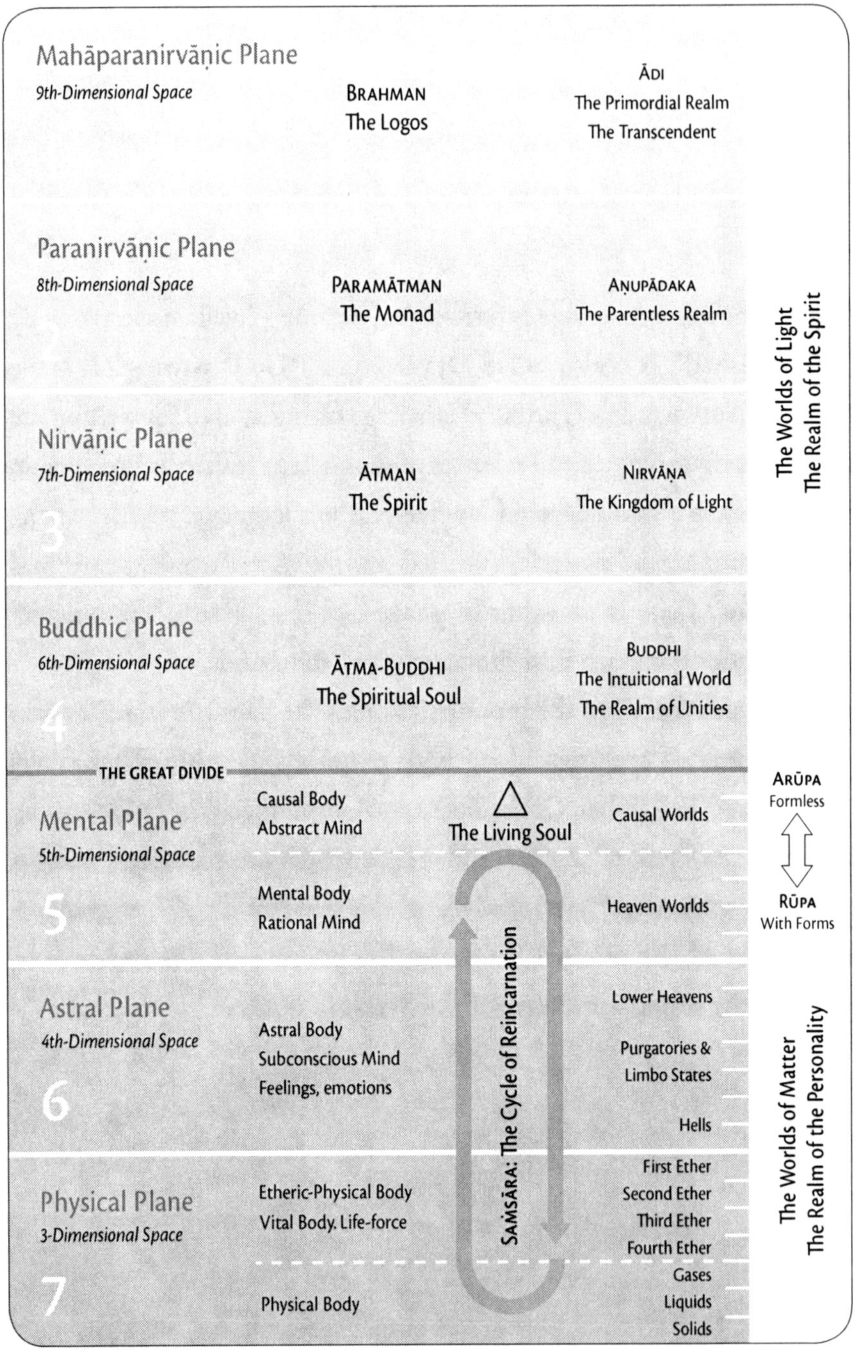

The Seven Great Planes of Being

PART I

The New Heaven and the New Earth

The Twenty-First Century and the Destiny of Mankind

The twenty-first century is a very crucial time for the destiny of Mankind[1] and the evolution of our planet.

In my book *Planetary Transformation* (and its companion book *The New Planetary Reality: The Coming Avatāra and the Nine Paths to Enlightenment)*, I gave the esoteric side of the planetary transformation we will be going through in the twenty-first century. When you begin to realize the tremendous problems of Humanity, however, you also need to have some solutions as to what to do about them. So those books offer a complete science of transformation with which you can completely change your life, including dozens of practical techniques to overcome the problems of day-to-day living amid the tremendously chaotic transformation which we are about to experience.

But now we are going to look at this whole process of planetary transformation in a different way because things are moving so fast on the planet that the crisis point is fast approaching. Forget everything the politicians or the economists tell you—the story is much bigger than that, infinitely larger. Hopefully, this book will help you understand the bigger story, which I have reduced to the following ten points.

1. Use of this word is explained in my book *Heavens and Hells of the Mind,* vol. i, p. xvii (Sounding-Light Publishing, 2007): "Throughout this book, the words *Man* and *Mankind* are used in their classical sense. *Man* is an Old English (Teutonic) word, synonymous with the Latin HOMO and the Hebrew ADAM, which means 'a human being, a human creature', as distinct from plant life, animal life, or angelic life on this planet. The word *Man* refers to the human species ... of both male and female genders."

1. Esoteric History

Firstly, what you see happening on the planet and what the historians have written about planetary history are only superficial phenomena. In other words, the normal understanding of history is like the observation of wavelets on the surface of an ocean or lake when the wind is blowing. Historians look at the world wars, the past civilizations of Greece, Rome, Egypt, China, and so on, and they write their theories and ideas about them. That is just the outer surface of history. There is another history we call *esoteric history*—history as it really happened and as it really happens. And that means we have to go to the bottom of the ocean, or as deep as possible, not just tinkle with the little waves dancing on the surface. The depth of the ocean, the depth of Reality, contains the real power.

So there is another layer of history only known to people who are esotericists, like the Yogīs, Sūfīs, Mystics and Saints of all religions, people who have had some inner spiritual experiences, who are born with higher levels of consciousness, with *inner* knowledge, and have a different idea of history. We will touch on that other side of history to convey to you some understanding of what is happening in the twenty-first century and what human destiny is because it is not what it appears to be; it is much more complex and you cannot understand it by following social or political theories that only touch the surface.

At the end of the last century many people thought that the end of the world was coming, that the Christ would return or that there would be a Golden Age. Of course that did not come about. Nowadays it is prognosticated that on 21 December 2012[2] a big transformation will take place and Humankind will live happily ever after. That too

2. In this case the author's prognostication of course turned out to be correct—these words were spoken during a talk delivered on 29 September 2012. (Ed.)

will not happen. There is another prognostication that the Avatāra has already come and that by the end of 2012 there will be a sufficient number of enlightened people so that the planet will enter the Golden Age. That will not happen either. What I'm trying to tell you is that all these prognostications are not based on the Esoteric Knowledge, which can only be perceived from within, from a higher level of consciousness, so such prognostications never come about.

So what is going to happen? Well, it is a complex situation and we will try to explain it by going back a long way in history, to the beginning of Creation. We start at the beginning because unless you understand basic fundamentals you will never understand the struggle of the planet over this and the next two or three centuries and what we can do about this struggle.

2. *Invisible Worlds, Realms, Forces and Conditions*

In order to understand the coming changes, you have to be aware that there are invisible worlds, realms, forces and conditions influencing the destiny of Mankind.

I was born with another kind of consciousness, with perceptions of higher realities, and for about the first twenty years of my life I was taught in the Inner Worlds all the time. It was an instruction from within, about the various planes of being, the different kinds of beings there, the structure of the Cosmos, and so on. If you were born with a higher level of consciousness like I was, or if you have had some mystical, spiritual or yogic experiences, or even some psychic experiences, you know that there are invisible worlds and realms, invisible forces and conditions.

This has to be understood: *we are actually living in invisible worlds.*

This Physical World is *within* another layer or dimension[3] of the space-time continuum that is called the Astral World or the Subtle World; which is within another world called the Mind dimension, the Mental World or Heaven World; which is in another dimension called the Buddhic World, the World of Unity; which is in yet another dimension called Nirvāṇa, the Absolute Field of Light, and so on up to cosmic heights—worlds within worlds within worlds.[4]

Consider that you are totally surrounded by invisible realms, a vast field of invisible energy. There is an infinite ocean of Matter-Energy-Spirit and there are currents moving in this ocean that touch Humanity, affecting *you* and the whole planetary structure. Within the Astral World, which is the next dimension above us, there are forces and conditions that are moving and changing, and all of these changes will have an impact on us. In the same way as the thoughts you think and the emotions you feel come out in your actions, whatever takes place in the invisible worlds will come out into reality as physical actions, events and situations. We have to respond to the activity within the invisible worlds, whether we like it or not, and that will change the way history develops, not only this year but over the next three centuries.

So one of the factors we have to consider regarding Mankind's destiny in this century is the function of the invisible worlds, and how those invisible forces work themselves out into physical manifestation is an *unknown* factor. This is why I say that you cannot predict exactly what is going to happen tomorrow or at the end of this century or the next few centuries. There has never been a situation where such dynamic changes will take place as this particular situation in this

3. In spiritual language we use the word *dimension* in terms of a realm, world or plane of being, not the mathematical or scientific definition of *dimension*.

4. See the diagram *The Seven Great Planes of Being* at the front of this book.

century. It's not going to be easy but the outcome could be more than our wildest dreams of utopia or a golden age. But first of all you have to acknowledge that invisible worlds and realms, invisible forces and conditions *are acting on us now.*

So, we acknowledge that there is another vast, unknown side of history, of which the average person is not aware, and which has to do with invisible worlds that have been influencing Mankind for millions of years and are acting on us now. There is also something that may happen in this century which could be a colossal, wonderful event. There is something gearing up in the invisible dimensions, and we will explain later on what might happen and how we can respond to it properly.

I hope that you can feel what I'm saying as an internal reality because I do not philosophize; I talk from inner experience. To me, these things are *real.*

3. *War in Heaven, Hierarchies, Good and Evil Powers*

The history of this planet is ancient. You may have heard of the Great War mentioned in scriptures that took place in Heaven long, long ago, when the good angels fought the bad angels. What has this to do with us now? Everything.

At the beginning of Creation, at the dawn of the MANVANTARA billions of years ago when the Divine Plan was still functioning correctly, there was a split in the unity of Creation. The Original Plan in the Divine Mind was that all the spiritual species would go out from the beautiful Worlds of Light (Nirvāṇa and the planes above) and slowly descend through the various layers of Creation into the physical dimension and go through the physical-world experience of the human species. However, some Spirits refused to do this. Why? You can imagine that to exist in Nirvāṇa or a higher cosmic plane would be quite an amazingly beautiful existence, a billion times better than here. So they said, "Why go down and immerse ourselves in matter? We would have to have physical bodies and because of those bodies we would have limitation and suffering." These were the so-called Fallen Angels, who were actually quite wise.

The Divine Plan is in the Mind of the Logos, the Cosmic Creator, but there is also freedom of will in the Cosmos. It is not that the angels were bad, but in using their free will they decided that they were not going to go through this long experience of millions of years of devolution and then millions of years of evolution. So they rebelled against the Divine Plan—and then there was a big war in Heaven.

This war was significant for the history of the Universe, the history of our Solar System and the history of Humanity because for the first time there was a disagreement, a split, in the Unity. At the dawn of Creation there was no division, no antagonism, no sense of separation, only the absolute state of Unity, Oneness and Cohesion. The rebellion of the angels created a division, and that split in the Unity has remained throughout the whole process of involution into matter. So there is now a cosmos with opposing energies or forces, with opposing hierarchies, with good and evil powers.

These good and evil powers are very important because they are working on this planet *now*. There are good hierarchies working for human evolution or advancement, and there are bad hierarchies who do not want Humanity to move onto the next level. Do not regard this as a philosophy, a theology or some religious dogma. No, it is a hundred percent correct fact: *there are evil powers that want to stop the evolution of Mankind.* These hierarchies want crystallization; they want everything to stay exactly how it is. Why? It is in their interest, which is to control this world. They rebelled a long time ago and they are still rebelling against change. Unless you take this into consideration you won't understand the *real* history of the planet, nor what is happening now or what will happen in this century. These good and bad forces continually acting on Humanity are in part determining what we are going to go through this century and what our destiny is. And what is the destiny of Mankind? We have to fight the evil powers.

By *evil* we do not mean they are evil in the normal sense of the word; they simply have another agenda. It is the agenda of some hierarchies to move *with* the force of the Original Plan of Creation, which is *in*volution (into matter) and *e*volution (back to the Spirit), and there are some hierarchies whose agenda is to go into matter and remain within the structure of matter. They do not want to move out of it and will oppose anybody who does want to move out of it.

You have to understand that when something good happens on the planet there is a force that opposes it. This also happens inside you, in your family and in all groups. Whenever human beings come together they are split in all directions, which is the work of the good and the evil powers. It is something cosmic, and if you do not understand this you will be totally puzzled about what is going on and why things happen the way they do.

In the New Testament, Saint Paul says, "For we are fighting not against humans, but against principalities and powers, against the rulers of the darkness of this world" (*Ephesians* 6: 12). *Principalities* is an ancient word for "hierarchies". In other words, Saint Paul was telling the early Christians, that they were not fighting the rulers of Israel at that time—they were nothing—they were fighting real hierarchies, evil powers that want to obstruct evolution, that want to stop the Light from expressing itself and becoming the Way for Humanity.

Every time you work for the Light the opposition comes. From practical experience I have had much opposition in my lifetime. The opposing forces have tried to put me out of action many times—physically, emotionally, mentally, spiritually, in every way. They work against you in any way they can because you bring in Light, you bring in Knowledge and Wisdom.

So if you want to have a clear picture of what will happen in this century, it's important to understand that there are several hierarchies, some good (they work for us) and some bad (they work against us). That is why we cannot say that it will be all good, it will be all bad, it will be all this or all that. It is a very complex situation.

4. *Kosmokratores (the Builders) and Dhyāni-Chohans (Spiritual Hierarchies)*

In ancient Greek, Kosmokratores means the "Builders", "those who build the Cosmos". They are a class of angelic or spiritual beings on the higher planes who build planets and star systems, worlds, planes and universes. At the beginning of a creation cycle they come into action and start building, first the higher worlds and then the lower worlds right down to the Physical World. Now, the problem is that they only *build* the Cosmos; that's their job. There is no morality or philosophy behind what they do. And this is part of the major problem on the planet in this century (or in any century): the Builders only built the physical structure of planet Earth; they didn't think of turning the planet into a spiritual heaven world or a nirvana. They did their job as builders, working with substance and matter to build the structure of the "house" we live in. They did not help our evolution because they themselves have nothing to do with Evolution.

Then there is another hierarchy, the Dhyāni-Chohans (which means the "Meditative Lords"), who are spiritual beings in the

Nirvāṇic World and above. They also are not able to help us because they do not function anywhere near our level of existence, just as the birds have no interest in what the fish do at the bottom of the ocean.

So there are entities who concentrate only on matter and entities who are totally above matter, and the two will never meet. And this dichotomy has existed in Humanity right from the beginning as the ongoing struggle between materialism and our aspiration to attain Nirvāṇa, or Liberation, because we respond partially to the Builders and partially to the Dhyāni-Chohans. Some part of human nature is always physical, because the Builders built our bodies out of matter, but some part of human nature, a spark of Divinity within us, belongs to the Dhyāni-Chohans. This dichotomy, the feeling of a split between Matter and Spirit, will increase as the century moves forward, unless we know how to bridge the gap—which is precisely what the whole field of Esoteric Science is about.

5. *Kalpas (Great Cycles of Time), Natural Disasters and Atlantis*

It is important to have some perspective on what is happening in this century. The planet has existed for billions of years and will exist for billions of years more; the Solar System has existed for billions of years and will exist for billions of years more; and the Universe has existed for billions of years and will exist for billions of years more. The Universe moves in huge cycles of time (Kalpas), with lesser cycles of time within them, and the irresistible forces of time push the planet and the Solar System (including Humanity) forward according to a certain cosmic *plan*.

At the moment people are taken up with natural disasters, which are happening everywhere, and of course the scientists say they are caused by global warming. Well, that may be true, but we have had natural disasters all the time. Global warming has taken place hundreds of times previously, along with hundreds of ice ages. In other words, the poles shift, continents rise, continents fall, and this has been going on for millions of years.

Natural disasters are part of the great cycles of time. Because human beings are so insignificantly small we think that all of these natural disasters—hurricanes, tornadoes, floods and heat waves—are end-of-the-world scenarios, but if you go back in history they have happened over and over again. Natural disasters are part of the reaction of Nature to cosmic happenings, as the planet swirls around the Sun and the Sun swirls around other Suns and other points of energy in the Cosmos. The poor old planet is reacting and sometimes the reaction is very severe, like during the Lemurian and Atlantean Ages. The planet is trying to rid itself of certain unwanted energies and therefore we experience cataclysms.

You might think that all of this bad weather is a sign that God does not love us or that there is some kind of a conspiracy, but you have to understand it as a cosmic occurrence. When a natural disaster occurs, just think that our Mother Earth is reacting to cosmic forces and there is no other way for her to react. Take it in stride, think of it as a positive event and see what you can do about the situation, how you can help yourself and how you can help other people. That is why you have to have peace of mind. When you understand the cause of things, you will never lose your peace of mind, in spite of all the tremendous happenings on this planet.

Another important consideration is Atlantis. Much of what the planet and Humanity are experiencing now, and will experience over the next centuries, started in Atlantis, which was located between the Pacific and Atlantic Oceans and encompassed the United States and a part of Europe. Humanity was already having problems during Atlantean days, when people knew how to control Nature and nature-spirits, and how to control the Astral World and astral energies. Unfortunately they misused that knowledge and more than half the population of Atlantis turned into black magicians, and this started the problems that we have now.

In Atlantean days there were major wars that were nothing like the wars we have today. War to us nowadays is about blowing things up, but the Atlanteans were more refined: they could wage war with their minds, creating tremendous mental, emotional and psychic forces that split Humanity into good and bad magicians. Many of the Atlantean magicians are incarnating now—the first wave started returning in 1875—and this century will see many more old Atlanteans returning, both good and bad—that is, those who control negative energies and forces and those who try to work with the Light Forces.

So human beings are now exposed to these dual forces: those who are working *for* the Forces of Light and those who want to *obstruct* the Forces of Light. (The influence of the latter will unfortunately increase as the century goes on.) This is where you come in, because you have to understand and acknowledge that this is happening and then decide which side you are on. This is explained in the following quote from the synopsis of my book *Planetary Transformation*. "In the turbulent days to come, people will have a choice: Be one of those who are buffeted by events they do not understand. Or be one of those who know what is happening and who will work with the incoming energy of change to help turn planet Earth into an unimaginable world of Harmony, Love, Peace and Unity."

In other words, you unfortunately have to *know* before you can *do*. It is important that you look at all these events calmly and understand their causes and what you can do about them, because millions of people will be swept up by energies and forces they do not comprehend, as they are even now. If you observe Humanity you see that many people are like leaves blown hither and thither in the wind. Look at all the things that are happening in the world now: people marching and protesting without the slightest understanding that they are being influenced and manipulated by invisible forces, without understanding the larger picture of what is happening on this planet.

So we are going to have a lot of karma to work out from the time of Atlantis. This century is going to be quite troublesome because the Atlantean magicians coming back have psychic powers, and since they cannot change their material ambitions, we will have to battle them to liberate the planet. It is all part of the story of this twenty-first century.

6. *Materialism and Science*

The danger of materialism is its spiritual ignorance, because materialism presumes that only matter exists. Science is *very* materialistic; it believes that only this physical universe exists, and that's it!

This is an incredible drag on human consciousness that helps keep it in materiality. Many people worship science and think that it has all there is that can be known. That's bad enough, but one more danger is scientific experimentation, especially what scientists are doing in Europe, smashing atoms together in the Large Hadron Collider.

This has to be understood from the point of view of *esoteric* science, not physical science. Every layer of Space has an atomic structure that separates it from the next layer. Expressed in esoteric language, the physical dimension, or Physical World, has an atomic layer, what we call the *etheric web*, which is a layer of atoms that prevents the forces and energies of the Astral World from intruding into the physical dimension. Similarly, there are layers of atoms between the astral and the mental dimensions, between the mental and the Buddhic dimensions and between the Buddhic and the Nirvāṇic dimensions. In other words, the layers of atoms are like separating walls between the dimensions. If all the forces of the various dimensions were impacting on each other in all directions without any control, there would be no structure and we would be back in the Original Chaos. The whole purpose of the layers of atoms is to keep things in compartments so they can function as they are meant to, by evolutionary plan or purpose.

The scientists, in their ignorance, are smashing atoms to ever-smaller particles, pursuing an intellectual idea of finding the smallest particle, but they are actually damaging the etheric web, the etheric structure of the planet. Each time they run an experiment with their powerful beams, they weaken the planet's atomic structure. It's like punching holes in a bucket: after a while the holes are big enough that the bucket isn't a bucket any more. They may not blow themselves up in the process because they are clever enough to be able to control their machine, but what they do not understand is that the atomic layer of the planet is intelligent and has its own purpose. You can't keep smashing it just to satisfy some scientific curiosity that has nothing to do with the nature of the planet, which has to be protected from the high-velocity energies of the inner dimensions. People are worried about ozone holes, but if scientists manage to make a big hole in the etheric web, it will be infinitely more dangerous.

If that happens there will be an inflow of astral forces and energies throughout Europe. People will be exposed to all kinds of energies, entities and forces that they do not understand and can't control. The scientists have no idea that other things may exist beyond their theoretical ideas. They think they have to prove, or not prove, that this or that particle exists, but they do not actually *do* anything, at least nothing of practical value. The amazing thing is that nobody controls them; no government or international organization asks whether what they are doing has any real purpose behind it.

What they are doing is a destructive activity based on absolute ignorance of the structure of the atom, the structure of the planet, the structure of the Universe. Scientists think the atom is just an unintelligent mass or energy but what they do not realize is that atoms are intelligent entities and when they destroy them they are destroying intelligent entities. In their own world, atoms are just as significant as the human species on this planet, except they are on a very minute scale. But on their level they are not minute; they are minute to us in the same way as we are minute and insignificant compared to a star system or galaxy.

I mentioned before[5] that within the next three hundred years the astral dimension may merge with the physical dimension, but that will occur through the Light of the Buddhic World absorbing the Astral World and pushing it down towards the physical dimension. Now that would be a *divine intervention*, part of the Divine Plan, and very different from what the scientists are ignorantly doing. I'm not saying that a disaster will happen but it is a possibility unless they shut their machine down. No human being, unless very highly trained, will be able to deal with all the incoming astral energies.

I'll give you an example of how astral energies work on a personal level. Many years ago, in the 1960s and 1970s, when people were experimenting with LSD and all sorts of combinations of drugs, I would be asked to help people who had reached a bad end on drugs. There was one group of university students who knew that I had inner

5. Imre Vallyon, "Interdimensional Change", in *Planetary Transformation* (Sounding-Light Publishing, 2010), 25–36.

knowledge and asked me to find out what happens to them when they take drugs. So one night I stayed with them while they took their drugs. It was the following afternoon before they had recovered sufficient rationality that I could tell them exactly what happened to them.

What I observed in them was that when they took a drug it punctured their etheric body. Just as the planet has an etheric web, we each have an etheric part of the physical body made of etheric atomic matter that prevents the astral body from merging directly into the physical body. This is necessary because if the astral body directly merged with the physical body, we would be astrally conscious and wouldn't be able to focus on this world at all, which would cause insanity and many other problems. So I told them, "Look, what I saw is that you have many holes in your etheric body and if you continue doing this you will likely become insane because you will not be able to control the astral energies pouring into your system." They never took any more drugs after that.

7. Astrological Influences on Countries and Their Leaders and Politicians

Every country is influenced by certain cosmic influences that come under astrological influences, but not only the countries come under these influences but also their leaders and politicians. If you look at some of the major events on this planet, like the French Revolution, the Russian Revolution, the First World War and the Second World War, and if you look at the astrological influences on the countries involved, you can see that there were definite reasons for those events, and you can also see influences in the astrological charts of the leaders of those countries. So there is a connection between the astrological influence on a country and the influence on its leadership.

If a country's chart indicates war but the leadership is totally positive, then there will be no war. But when the astrological chart of a country corresponds with the leader's chart and they are both on the destructive line, then there will be war. That was the case with the First World War, the Second World War and the French and Russian Revolutions. They were caused by certain astrological influences and their leaders were responding to those influences because their own personal charts had the same influences.

At the moment, China is on the rise. Starting since around 1948, China has been steadily increasing its power and is now influencing Southeast Asia, Africa, the Pacific Islands and even Eastern European countries. As long as the leadership has a relatively neutral astrological chart, China will just keep building up its economic power and influence, but without going to war. But if one leadership group comes in that is charged with war, China *will* go to war. And that would be the next major disaster, even worse than the Second World War.

And another big thing is religious war. If you study the history of the Muslim religion, you know that after the Prophet Mohammed established the Muslim religion it split into two: the Shia and the Sunni, who have been fighting and persecuting one another ever since. These two sects have created problems in Iraq, Syria, Afghanistan and other countries in the Middle East for many centuries. But another problem is that the Muslim religion itself is against the rest of the world, and many Muslims have the idea that they want to conquer the world by religion. This has been simmering for many centuries and it may be precipitated sooner or later. So one possibility is an all-out war in the Middle East between the two big factions of the Muslim religion, or the two Muslim sects may join against Christianity or the rest of the world.

8. *Free Will and Conditioning by Religion, Politics, Science, Culture, Tradition*

Another big problem we are facing is the blocking of free will by *conditioning*. Every one of us has free will; every human being is born *free*. Every human being, however, becomes conditioned by family, environment, religion, politics, science, culture and tradition, and this is another problem that has to be solved this century. For instance, if you are conditioned by religion, you will like your religion and hate the other religions. If you are conditioned by politics you will be a communist or a capitalist or whatever. And many people are conditioned by science, which, as I said, is materialistic and conditions people to think materialistically.

This conditioning overlays your free will, so before you can be of any help to Humanity you first have to re-establish your free will. You have to divest yourself of what you learned from your religion, school, culture or tradition and ask yourself, "Who am I? Where is my free will?" If you observe yourself, most of the time you are doing what you have been conditioned to do, without any free will whatsoever. You cannot choose to be a servant of the Light or a Warrior of Light while you are conditioned. You have to get rid of all your conditioning and become a free person. Being a free person means that you are an independent, free spirit in the Cosmos. Then the forces of Light will notice you and you will be able to work for them.

9. *Divine Intervention, the Spiritual Hierarchy, the Avatāra and the Divine Plan*

After having heard all these bad things, you might say, "Oh my God, there's no hope for Mankind!" It might seem like that but Mankind has not been left by itself to solve all these tremendous problems, most of which are cosmic and beyond our scope anyhow. Now, we also have Divine Intervention acting through the Spiritual Hierarchy.[6]

Over the millions of years since Humankind came into existence, from all the religions, those who have become Saints, Adepts, Yogīs or spiritually realized people have formed an invisible hierarchy that we call the *Spiritual Hierarchy*. This hierarchy has always been functioning—in the past through the Mystery Schools of Egypt, Rome, Greece, Persia, China, Babylonia, all over the ancient world, including Atlantis, and in the Ashram system of India, where a particular Guru, Master or Teacher taught the Esoteric Science.

So the Spiritual Hierarchy has been in existence for a long time but the difference now is that because of this critical time in the evolution of the planet—you could say it is the most critical time ever—the possibility of transforming this planet into a spiritual planet is very real and close. And because of that the Spiritual Hierarchy has decided to step up and be a little more active. This means that nowadays the influence of the Hierarchy will not be through one particular school or one particular person; rather, the Hierarchy will try to spread its influence over the whole planet.

Corresponding to this understanding is the understanding of the Avatāra. In the olden days an Avatāra was a single manifestation, an embodiment of a divine state of being, like the Buddha, the Christ, Kṛṣṇa, Rama, Lao Tzu, Quan Yin or Isis. Each Avatāra embodied a certain cosmic principle: the Christ embodied Love; Kṛṣṇa embodied Devotion; Rama embodied Discipline, Law and Order; Lao Tzu embodied Wisdom; and Buddha embodied Enlightenment. They all

6. This topic is discussed in more detail in: Imre Vallyon, "The Mystery of the Coming Avatāra" in *The New Planetary Reality: The Coming Avatāra and the Nine Paths to Enlightenment* (Sounding-Light Publishing, 2012), 7–38.

brought certain qualities into human consciousness, coming down from the Spiritual Hierarchy—*Avatāra* means "one who descends"—to bring a particular energy stream to Humanity.

The difference now is that the Avatāra is not going to manifest in that way at all. Every religion has the idea of an Avatāra coming back but every religion thinks that the Avatāra will be one person who comes back to *their* religion. The Christians say the Christ will come back to them, the Buddhists say Lord Maitreya will come back to them and the Muslims say the Imam Mahdi will come back to them. But it's not going to be like that at all. Now the Avatāra is something much vaster, on a planetary scale.

The Avatāra coming to the planet now is a multidimensional reality. It will include individual entities, as well as the possibility of transforming planetary consciousness itself. In other words, the Avatāra will be an energy-field of Light embracing and penetrating the whole planet, and within that massive field of Light there will be points of Light which could be individual Avatāras—great Gurus, Teachers, Saints or Masters coming down to participate in the Work. But the main thing is that the Avatāra is not just for the Christians or for the Jews, it is not one person who is going to save one nation or one religion; it is a global event.

The influence of the Avatāra will become stronger and stronger as the Spiritual Hierarchy becomes more active and fuses the Avatāric energy. The Avatāra is *not* the Spiritual Hierarchy; you have to understand that they are two different things. The Spiritual Hierarchy is a kind of Group Soul consisting of many thousands of enlightened people, but the Avatāra is a cosmic energy, and as I said, the Hierarchy will make use of it for planetary enlightenment. So the influence of the Avatāra is already happening and you will see its manifestation in inspired teachers bringing in Esoteric Knowledge, who will be coming into incarnation more frequently from now on. They are simply fulfilling a part of the Divine Plan that is very ancient, that has existed since the Foundation of the World. That Plan has always been there but now it is going to be worked on much more intelligently.

10. Your Task Is to Bring Esoteric Knowledge to Mankind

This is an amazing century, an important century, a high mark in the history of the planet that will make or break us. Either we will go over to the Light or we will go back to the Dark Ages again. Don't forget that there are the opposing forces that will try to take us back to the Dark Ages, so the more you understand, the more you can fight ignorance and materialism with the forces of Light.

The important point is that Mankind will not be abandoned. The Spiritual Hierarchy is there to help us but they cannot help unless we *want* their help. There is a law in the Cosmos that the higher hierarchies cannot force their Light, their Energy, their Vibration onto the lower hierarchies—unlike the evil forces, which have no laws and force their energy on us, not even considering that they should not influence people. The Spiritual Hierarchy only works by request. They see the Light shining inside you, in your Head and in your Heart, and they may stimulate it a little, but they cannot take over your mind. That is their handicap.

So my message to you is simple: be a Warrior of Light. Then you will be able to help the planet go through this amazing century. We can be victorious and we can turn this planet into the most amazing hub of civilization that could ever possibly be imagined. You have to teach others in whatever way you can. The main thing is that you have Light in your consciousness, and that Light will help you know what to do. Remember when Jesus was going to be crucified He sent His disciples out to go and teach everybody, and one of the apostles asked, "But Master, what do we say?" Jesus said, "Don't worry. The Spirit will speak through you, the Spirit will act through you, so long as you align yourself with the Forces of Light" (*Matthew* 28: 19; *John* 14: 26).

The New Heaven and The New Earth

Introduction

We have to start with deeper knowledge—THEOSOPHIA, Divine Wisdom—before we can understand the real story behind the planetary events that are going on. First of all, you have to understand that what we see, the whole physical Universe, is only the *skin* of the multidimensional Universe. This planet Earth is only the skin of the planet Earth. Behind that is the flesh, behind that is the bone, behind that is the marrow, and so on. In other words, what you see is only a fragment of Reality.

If you are not used to this idea that there are things beyond what you see, consider this: *You* are an invisible entity. Your emotional structure is invisible, your mind-structure is invisible, your Soul is invisible, the Spirit within the Soul is invisible and the Deity within the Spirit is invisible. The *real* things are in the invisible dimensions. The Soul is eternal and the Spirit is eternal; your body lives only seventy years or so, and then it's kaput, useless, gone. (Even your mind and emotions continue after death.)

Consider yourself: every time you *feel* something there is a change in the chemistry and atomic substance of your physical body; every time you *think* something there is a change in your physical body; every time you *act* or do something there is a change in your physical body. And whenever there are changes in the Inner Worlds, there are changes in the physical body of the planet, *which is the world we live in*. What happens to you on a small scale happens to the planet on a larger scale, to the Solar System on an even larger scale and to the Galaxy on a cosmic scale. The same Law rules in ever-greater circles. In other words, there is always an innermost point that starts off the reality that manifests on the physical dimension. The problem with the sociologists and scientists who theorize about what's happening on the planet is that they consider only the physical, but that has nothing to do with cause; it's already a result.

So it is from the inner realms where the problems, or the changes, arise, and how they work out in the physical dimension is where Humanity comes in. Humanity does not cause anything; we are the end result. But, it's how we react to the Inner Reality that organizes our life in the Physical World; it's how we react that determines human destiny. Human destiny is not a haphazard thing, not something uncontrolled or uncontrollable. It is exactly what human beings make it. That's all. If we make a mess of it, well, that's our destiny. If we react correctly, then we will have a Golden Age. Wars and disasters occur because we react wrongly to the energies coming in. It's very simple.

And this is where the whole art and science of Esoteric Wisdom comes in. You have to have inner spiritual vision or mystical experiences or training in the Esoteric Science. If you just have a worldly interpretation you will never understand what is really going on. It's just not possible. As I said, you cannot understand things simply by what the meteorologists say, what the scientists say, what the sociologists say. They are far from spiritual understanding, and they will be until they consider the vast Invisible Reality.

So I will describe ten *causes* and ten *results* of the coming changes, dividing the subject into two parts: the new Heaven and the new Earth. It says in the New Testament that there will be a new Heaven and a new Earth (*Revelations* 21: 1). When these colossal changes of the planet come about, there *will* be a new Heaven and a new Earth. We will start with the new Heaven because in order to understand why everything is happening as it is, we have to start at the top, in the invisible worlds, where the origins and causes of things are.

The New Heaven

In ancient days, in the ancient Greek, Hebrew and Aramaic languages, the word for *heaven* didn't just mean "the sky"; it had other meanings: "a dimension", a world, an inner reality". So when they said that there would be a new Heaven in this great transfiguration of the planet, they didn't mean that we would have a new sky. A "new Heaven" referred to new Inner Worlds, new events happening in the inner part of the planet, the inner part of the Solar System, the inner part of the Cosmos.

The following are the real causes that explain why the planet is as it is, the real causes of the upheavals that the planet will have to go through for the next thousand years.

1. The Changes in the Inner Worlds

Most religions have the idea that there is *this* world and there is the *next* world—a heaven world or a nirvana or somewhere you go to after you die. Most people believe in an afterlife, but they have a rigid idea of what that afterlife is. In the Christian idea of Heaven, for example, it is a static place where the Father, Son and Holy Spirit exist, where you go after you have died if you've been good. If you haven't been good, well, bad luck, you go to the hell worlds (which are also unchangeable), where Lucifer and his minions will prod you with sticks. But the main idea is that Heaven and Hell (the Inner Worlds) are *fixed*, that you go from here to there, and that's it. But that isn't it. The Inner Worlds are not fixed; in fact, that's where the changes originate.

The first change is always in the Divine Will, and the level of Creation where the Divine Will first expresses an idea or a plan is what Buddha called *Nirvāṇa* or what the Christ called the *Kingdom of God.* We're talking about God on the Solar Systemic scale, not on the Absolute level, but that part of God that manifests in our Solar System. Any change that is to take place in the Solar System exists first in the Divine Mind, the Mind of the Deity of our Solar System, whom we call the *Solar Logos.* That change flashes across His Mind on the Logoic level and then hits the Nirvāṇic World, where action begins. It then slowly filters down through the dimensions until it manifests in the physical dimensions, the home of the lowest expression of the Deity. (The higher expressions are transcendental, way beyond Nirvāṇa, and we have no knowledge of them.)

So, over the next thousand years there will be changes in Heaven, in the Inner Worlds—changes in energy, vibration, colour schemes, structural schemes—and anybody who has inner vision or higher faculties will notice the changes.

2. *Angelic Hierarchies in the Physical World*

Those who are not into Esoteric Science think that angels are just a part of some nice mythology or that they are just for superstitious people. In actual fact, angels are beings who live in the Inner Worlds, but they are not of the human species. There are twelve Creative Hierarchies[7] in the Solar System: one of them is the Human Hierarchy, which

7. The twelve Creative Hierarchies are explained in diagram form in: Imre Vallyon, *Heavens and Hells of the Mind,* i. 191 (Sounding-Light Publishing, 2007).

we call the human species, and there are two Angelic Hierarchies.

The changes in the Inner Worlds are also affecting the Angelic Hierarchies in all the invisible dimensions, which are their natural habitats, and because of the changes within those worlds there is just as much upheaval in the Angelic Kingdom as in the Human Kingdom. Why? Because the angels have their own evolutionary plan, their own way of evolving in order to reach perfection, so they are also being forced to change to a new pattern. This change, however, also affects us, and the reason why has to do with the Angelic Hierarchies in the Physical World.

The physical world you see around you is only a fragment of the Physical World, the part composed of solids, liquids and gases. We can only sense dense solid and liquid substances, however; we cannot sense a gas unless it is pungent. But there are four etheric dimensions that are part of the Physical World that we do not sense at all. The Angelic Hierarchies in the Physical World live in these four etheric realms. They are still in the physical dimension but invisible because our five senses cannot register the etheric vibration. However, if you read the scriptures of various religions you will notice that these angels appear and do things in our world. That's because the angels in the etheric-physical dimension can densify enough to become visible and interact with humans.

So the whole angelic species has to undergo change, including the angels in the Physical World—who will begin to manifest physically. Part of the Divine Plan is that the Human Hierarchy and the Angelic Hierarchy will become one hierarchy at some time in the distant future, as part of the *New Earth*. Already, the angels closest to us in the etheric-physical dimension have begun to interact with us: Have you heard of UFOs? UFO appearances, which are manifestations from one of the four etheric dimensions, are simply ways the angels use of letting people know that they exist. Another way of communicating is trying to impress crop-circle designs on our consciousness. The beautiful crop circles are magical designs that the Angelic Hierarchy understands and uses to try to communicate to us the Divine Plan for planet Earth.

Notice that they are *trying* to communicate with us. The problem is, at this stage we cannot meet them face to face and work together as a team because of the extreme violence and aggression of the human species. There is no other species in the Universe that is as violent and aggressive as the human beings on this planet. *This is a planet of war!* If you look back at history: what have human beings done for the past million years? Kill each other. The history of the planet is nothing but a history of violence. For the angels, this is a handicap. They cannot approach us because they do not work through violence; they can only deal harmoniously with nonviolent beings.

The angels know the Plan because they see the Universe from within *out*, whereas we look at it only from the outside. They can see the inside of the planet Earth, the atoms and substances vibrating, and they can see how the human being is constituted. So they try with geometrical designs and patterns to tell us what the Plan is. But as I said, for them to appear physically or physically communicate with us cannot happen until human beings stop being so violent. Humans are afraid of communicating with anything nonhuman. In fact, they are afraid of communicating with each other! That's why there is so much fighting between countries.

One more way the angels try to communicate with us is through manifestations in the sky. During the First and Second World Wars there were reports of soldiers on both sides who saw huge flaming crosses or geometric patterns across the sky. Of course, many soldiers thought they were signs from God, but they were just the angels trying to show them what peace was and how they were destroying the planet.

This communication has been going on for centuries, but as I said there is still the problem of no direct communication because of our wrong nature. But that will slowly change. Over the next few hundred years you will see that angelic beings will be more able to communicate with us, and within one thousand years, hopefully, the two kingdoms—the angels of the Physical World and the humans of the Physical World—will be able to cooperate and work together. When that happens new human beings will be born who will be able to see from the inside out, and they will tell us how the energies work within, giving us technology and knowledge undreamed of at this time. When you see something from the inside out, you *know* how it works. So we will know the causes of diseases and how to cure them and the causes of natural disasters and what to do about them. That can happen—as soon as human beings are ready to give up their violent ways.

3. *New Light in the Astral World*

The next world beyond the Physical World is the Astral World, which is also called the psychic dimension or the after-death world, where people go after they die. Now, the Astral World has its own light by which the people living there can see, in the same way as the Physical World has light from the Sun. If you leave your body in meditation or after you go to sleep, you go to the astral dimension. You can move around and do things there, just like you do here, and you can see colours, shapes and objects, just like you see here, except that they are not lit by the Sun but by what we call the Astral Light, which is the radiance of the astral substance itself.

The problem is that the Astral World now has a new light. What this means is that people in the Astral World, people who are in the after-death state, are being shaken up because a new Light-Energy coming from a much superior dimension is bombarding and changing their world. It would be the same if the light of the Sun were becoming more intense as the days went by; that would obviously have a tremendous effect on the Physical World. Well, the light of the Astral World is increasing in intensity and everybody on the other side will have to change because their astral bodies (in which they live in the Astral World) will pick up the higher rates of vibration. So whether you live in this world or the next, you will have to change. Nobody will escape the changes on this planet.

The important thing to understand is that because the Astral Light is intensifying, human beings will be more sensitive. There will be more clairvoyant, clairaudient and clairsentient people, people who can see the future or have knowledge of the past. So within one or two hundred years, many people will be natural (not trained) psychics, and they will be able to pick up on the intensity of the faster Astral Light vibration. And here is the danger: if those psychic people do not have what we call Wisdom, or knowledge of the Esoteric Science, they can misinterpret what they see.

Psychics always think there is an all-important message from the Cosmos in whatever they see. It's usually not important; it's usually insignificant. They just see something that is going on in the Astral World, a thoughtform maybe or a colour or whatever. It doesn't mean that it is a world-shattering event. And that's where psychics need proper education in the spiritual sciences to understand what they see, whether it is valid or not, whether it is important or not, and if it is, what to do about it.

Anyhow, the Astral World is undergoing changes because the Astral Light is changing, and this adds to the problems the planet has to work through.

4. The Cyclic Nature of Energies and the Zodiac

Beyond our Solar System, the Cosmos is an infinite electromagnetic energy-field of *manifestation*. You could say that the Absolute, or the Infinite Mind, is a massive, immeasurable field of energy, but within that immeasurable field of energy there are cyclic movements and each movement is different. When the Wheel turns, a new energy-field comes and shakes up the inner dimensions of Reality. So, for example, when a new cyclic wave from the higher dimensions hits the energy-field of our Sun, it affects the whole radiation field of the Sun, which contains every planet and everything on it.

And this is another thing that is happening at the moment: a new wave of energy is hitting the energy-field of our Sun and intensifying every vibration in the Solar System, and because of that all of the planets in our Solar System are being impacted. That's number one.

Number two is that the Solar System is being influenced by another part of the zodiac. Now, you know that the last age was called the Piscean Age and now we are in the Aquarian Age. What this means is that our Sun and all its planets—which are only smaller energy-fields within the larger energy-field of the Sun itself—that whole vast living mechanism is coming under the influence of the constellation of Aquarius.

All the stars within each constellation of the zodiac emanate energy, and they have their unique energy-field. In fact, every planet and every star in the Cosmos has its unique energy-field according to its cosmic development, because—and this might stretch your mind a bit—every star and planet is a living being! Most people think that the Earth is just composed of dead matter that somehow got together and formed itself into a planet. They can't understand that there is *intelligence* behind everything—an atom is intelligent, a planet is intelligent, a star is intelligent, a cosmos is intelligent.

This means that we have two kinds of energies coming at us: the cyclic energies coming from the higher dimensions, from the Kingdom of God, or Nirvāṇa, and the Sun coming under the influence of a different star system. So we are bombarded by vertically moving energies from the *inside* and horizontally moving energies from the *outside*.

The combination of these energies will be extraordinary; the whole planet is going to vibrate faster and faster. And what will the human beings do? That is the problem. What they will do is start killing each other. When people are overstimulated they declare war on somebody so that they can blow off some steam. Remember, the way human beings behave is not compulsory; it's a choice. Nobody makes people kill each other; it's just how they react because of ignorance and their warped nature. Increased vibrations can actually be used for our benefit.

The two vibrations together form the Cross, which is actually a symbol of evolution, so the possibility for our evolution is phenomenal. In one hundred years we could become like the angels; in two hundred years, like the archangels; in one thousand years, like the ELOHĪM, the KOSMOKRATORES. There is no limit to what we can do. And it is all determined by how we react to things. Will we react negatively, and create devastation, or positively, and become Buddhas and Christs?

That is the whole point and that is why this is a tremendous opportunity. We had an opportunity like this in Lemurian times and we messed it up; and in Atlantean times we messed it up again. Unfortunately, when these great cyclical stimulations happen we tend to mess things up through ignorance and our unstable nature, and through *not wanting to change* with the new energies. That is the big thing: not wanting to change, holding on to the past. That has been the curse of human evolution for millions of years!

In reality, these are amazing opportunities for cosmic evolution. Really, really amazing! An opportunity like this only comes once every hundred thousand years or so. The zodiac changes every 2,160 years but it's very seldom that the internal cyclical energies come down at the same time as the zodiacal change. We are moving within and without simultaneously, so it's a phenomenal chance for growth, for the speeding up of the evolution of all life on this planet.

5. *The Return of the Christ (the Energy of Love, Unity and Oneness)*

If things aren't complicated enough—what with dealing with all the energies from the Angelic Hierarchy and the Astral Light changes and all the energies from the inner cyclic and zodiacal changes—we have another problem: the Christ Himself. Those of you who are Christians believe there was a person called Jesus Christ who died on the cross and then resurrected and went to Heaven.

Actually, the Christ is a highly evolved entity, way ahead of normal human evolution; His aura is large enough to embrace the whole planet. So when He incarnated as a human two thousand years ago it was for a planetary purpose: to stimulate the evolution of the human species. He brought in an energy, a vibration we call the energy of Love, Unity and Oneness. The Christ stimulated people with that energy, talking about forgiveness, loving your neighbour, and so on, because we are one family and there is only one Father in Heaven. That's the energy of Oneness, the energy of Love.

After the Christ died He went up the various planes and stationed Himself in what we call the Kingdom of God (Nirvāṇa). Now He is coming down through the Buddhic World, the Causal World, the Mental World, the Astral World and will finally incarnate in the Physical World. Now that causes another problem, as you can imagine, because as He descends through the various levels He is introducing the powerful vibration of Love, an energy of binding all the beings in those worlds together.

On this planet, the reaction to that will be colossal—colossally bad, that is!—because there are people who do not want to work together, who do not want the Love energy. They are crystallized and want to be separate; they do not want the nations to be united or Humanity to be united as one species. If that Love vibration were able to function on Earth, there would be no nations, just one planet, one Humanity, one religion, one Path, one Reality. That's the energy of Love, but as I said, there is also an opposite response to it from those who do not want Oneness and will fight against it tooth and nail. You can't exploit somebody if you are one with that person and you can't kill somebody if you are one with that person. The act of *uniting* requires a major change in consciousness, and people do not want that.

To give you a real-world example, the United Nations was originally supposed to be an organization for unity, but it has been blocked by the separatists. Russia was given the power of veto, which it has often used to veto democratic proposals, those that favour freedom of expression, and it tends to support dictatorships. China does the same. These powers strive to oppose freedom and they will cause more problems in the world, and that is to be expected.

The Christ is going to manifest physically but at the moment He is mainly working through Mystics, Esoteric Teachers, Initiates and other people who can respond to that Love energy. They are doing the preliminary education of the masses, finding people who are receptive to the idea that there is only one world and one Humanity, preparing the world for the Christ.

6. Divine Intervention

Unfortunately, human beings cannot distinguish between right and wrong, between the Forces of Light and the Forces of Darkness. It is amazing to me that during the First and Second World Wars there were so many people who took the wrong side. For example, in the Second World War there was Nazi Germany, a total dictatorship; there was Stalin's Russia, a total dictatorship; and there was Japan, a total dictatorship; and there were the democratic countries of the West. But many people who took part in the war took the wrong side because they didn't know the difference between supporting dictatorship and supporting democracy and freedom of speech. They didn't know that there is right and wrong, that there is an evil power and a good power.

The movie *Star Wars* is a good example of this. It has Darth Vader, who represents the evil power, and Luke Skywalker, representing the good power. Now if you ask kids which one is their favourite, many will choose Darth Vader, the evil power. Right from childhood people cannot distinguish between a good force and a bad force, so when they grow up to be adults they will take the wrong side because they are lacking something inside them that is able to see that every evil force limits freedom—freedom of thought, religion, movement. They can't see the difference, until of course they are caught up in it.

I was brought up in a communist country, in Hungary, when Stalin was the head of Eastern Europe. I remember going once from Budapest to Vienna, which in those days was communist. At the train station in Vienna there were university students selling books on Marx and Engel and saying how wonderful communism was. They had no idea what a dictatorship does to people and how it works; they just read about the ideals of communism in their university books and supported it, which is very dangerous. There is a huge battle going on right now on this planet between the Forces of Light and the Forces of Darkness, and unfortunately people take the wrong side—and that stops the progress of the Forces of Light.

There is, however, the possibility of Divine Intervention, which has happened in the past and may happen now. During the First World War, the negative forces were winning, so one of the Angelic Hierarchies was asked to intervene and block the progress of the negative forces in the Inner Worlds by psychic energy. The same thing happened in the Second World War. Germany would have won the war but our Spiritual Hierarchy invoked help to block its energy on the Astral Plane. Once the energy was blocked, Hitler started making one mistake after another and finally lost the war. If Germany had won, there would be no free America, no free Australia or New Zealand, no free Asia. We would be back in the Dark Ages.

The World Wars were extreme emergencies and unless the positive forces received help we were going to be mired in dictatorships for a long time. So we were saved through Divine Intervention. But this does not mean we will be helped by Divine Intervention all the time, because by Cosmic Law human beings have free will. This means that we have to determine our own destiny; we cannot be babysat all the time. We must exercise our freedom, understand what is right and what is wrong, and make the right choices.

7. Planetary Karma and Atlantis

As a human being you have your own karma, which you accumulate life after life, and of course some of that karma has to be worked out in this lifetime, which is why you get sick or have accidents or other problems. Nobody, however, thinks that planet Earth has its own karma. As I mentioned previously, the planet is a living cosmic entity—call her Mother Earth if you like—and the physical planet is just her physical body, in the same way as we have a physical body. (She also has an astral body, mental body and causal body just like we have.) And Mother Earth also has *her* karma, which she accumulated through many incarnations. (The planets and the suns are great cosmic citizens that incarnate.)[8]

So Mother Earth has her own karma, which means that she is imperfect; she cannot control all the planetary energies in a totally harmonious way all the time. Can you control all of your thoughts and emotions in harmony all the time? No. Well, neither can our poor old Mother Earth. Now, if the planet were able to always harmonize the energies bombarding its radiation field, or auric energy field, then humans would have no other choice but to behave. But because planet Earth itself is struggling with all the new energies, there is a weakness that adversely affects all the kingdoms, including, of course, the human beings on the planet.

Planetary karma is one problem; another is the karma we accumulated when we were in Atlantis. The human karma from Atlantis is quite

8. The planets and suns are manifestations of the Cosmic Creator-Gods, who in the Old Testament are called the ELOHĪM. The following is a quote from my book *Heavens and Hells of the Mind,* iv. 1810 (Sounding-Light Publishing, 2007): "In *Genesis,* first appear the ELOHĪM, the male-female Creator-Gods, but the patriarchs did not like this fact because they wanted the work of all Creation to be done by only one Person. In later chapters it becomes ELOHĪM-JEHOVAH; then, by the time of Moses, it became JEHOVAH."

large because during that time we were quite naughty. The Atlantean civilization was highly scientific and it had a highly developed magic, so the Atlanteans were very good at using astral forces, cosmic forces and other invisible forces and energies against each other, waging war and killing each other. Unfortunately, this karma hasn't been forgotten and it's coming back now, as more and more Atlantean magicians are reincarnating and causing as much havoc as they can.

I'll give you an example. We had a meditation retreat in Europe a short time ago and one of my students who was not at the retreat sent me an email telling me that during the first five nights of the retreat she saw a brilliant light coming down onto the group attending the retreat—because she can see into the Astral World—but on the fifth night she saw five shining black objects and some entities dressed in black coming towards the energy-field of the group at the retreat. She instinctively decided to protect the group energy-field, so she put her hand up and invoked a Divine Name, which immediately released Light and made those objects disappear. If she hadn't done that, they would have penetrated the group energy-field and lowered its energy vibration or done some other damage.

In her email she asked, "Did I do right?" I wrote back and said, "Yes, you did, because the black figures travelling in those black objects are embodiments of the Dark Forces." I explained to her that these things happen all the time, that the war between Light and Dark is going on continually. Esoteric schools like ours are bombarded with negative energies on a regular basis. The Dark Forces try to destroy the school and the people who run it, because the esoteric groups work with Light energies.

8. The Christ Within You

There is the Christ, the cosmic being who is coming, as we mentioned before, but there is another Christ: the Christ within you. Within the Heart of every single human being, in the innermost part of the Soul, there is the Christ, quite literally. You have your physical body and within that is your etheric body, within that is your astral body, within that is your mental body, within that is your causal body, within that is your Soul and right within the Soul is the Christ—an image of Divinity made of pure Light, a Light entity that is *alive* but hidden in the deep regions of the Soul.

You can only step on the Spiritual Path when the Christ within you, which is a reflection of the Divine inside you, begins to sparkle at a higher frequency and shakes up your Soul and through your Soul sends down messages to you. Then you start to wake up and wonder: Who am I? What am I? Why am I here? That's because that Light impacts your Soul and then moves down and clarifies your mind and impacts your emotions and even your physical body. Now, if you want to be a Light-Worker, you have to *consciously* cooperate with the Christ within you.

So, how do you do that? Well, you have to meditate, you have to chant, you have to change your way of life, in other words, you have to go on the Spiritual Path. And that means reorganizing your whole life—your mind, emotions and physical activities—to fit in with the image of the Christ within you.

As you connect to the Christ within you, you begin to receive Light. First you receive the Light of Knowledge, whereby you begin to understand vaster things, cosmic realities, and you also understand certain events in your life and why they happened. You might even remember what happened in a past life or even have flashes of the future. Later on, after you have done lots of meditation and inner work, you will receive the Light of Life, a bright light, a pulsating White Brilliance you see in the Third-Eye Chakra or in the Crown Chakra. This Light is different from the Light of Knowledge, which is invisible but you know is there, working inside you; you simply understand cosmic principles. But when the Light of Life comes you literally *see* it like a radiance, a shining, luminous light, and you understand what it is. Then, as you keep working with the Christ within you, you become a Light-Worker and intelligently cooperate with everybody else who is working with the Light.

9. *Spiritual Regeneration Through Esoteric Knowledge*

People have to be taught that a human being is not just a physical body, that the causes of physical problems are not physical, that the planet is not just inert matter but has inner realities. They have to realize that they are responsible for their destiny; it cannot be left to chance or to somebody else. Without such knowledge, people experience results but do not know what caused them and therefore cannot change the situation. If you want to heal the sickness of the planet you have to know its cause. Before something can be done intelligently the causes must be known—and that requires Esoteric Knowledge, that is, *spiritual regeneration through Esoteric Knowledge.*

The Esoteric Science will save the planet and our job is to teach as many people as we can so that they know why things are as they are and what can be done about them. You can only change the planetary situation if you know which is the wrong side and which is the right side. As I said, even today people support the dictators, those who are actually anti freedom. And so long as we support the Negative Powers, the planet will be suffering as it does. That's why an esoteric education is all-important, and every group involved in this field should do its utmost to educate the public. There is good and bad in the world and we must be on the side of good. If we aren't, we'll just go on suffering century after century.

10. The Dangers of Materialism and Preconditioning

In the world today, materialism is almost total. You may know some people who are spiritual, but that's nothing. There are seven billion people who are materialistic, meaning that they are totally oriented towards their physical bodies and towards the physical world. Their main concern is to maintain their physical bodies and a good standard of living in the world. That is materialism, and everyone accepts it as normal. For example, when someone wins a gold medal in the Olympics they are treated as a hero. When they come home there are fireworks and society raves on about them because they won a gold medal by achieving something with their physical body. Everything that people do in the physical body is acknowledged and accepted by society. But society is not interested in those who excel in the spiritual field. The government doesn't call them up and give them a medal. Why? Because society is materialistic.

There is nothing wrong with materialism in itself. It's not a problem that people want to look after their bodies or make a good living. The problem is: *that's all they want to do in life; there is no spiritual counterbalance.* They completely negate the Soul and the Spirit within themselves. *That* is the problem.

At the moment, there is a clash between materialism (the body and the world) and the Soul or the Spirit. How many people are interested in the Spirit within them? How many are Soul-Conscious? If this clash is not resolved in the next three of four hundred years, we're going to have a dark age like never before. Everyone will be wallowing in material comfort, but the Soul within them will be absolutely dead.

It is a huge danger and people do not understand that overemphasizing materialistic values and not even mentioning spiritual values is a downward spiral of human and planetary evolution.

The Negative Powers make good use of the situation—they have a field day. Their whole purpose is to make people materialistic so that they become locked in this physical dimension. Since the time of Atlantis the Negative Powers have not wanted human beings to evolve, but have tried to keep them in servitude to material forces, material energies and material hierarchies. Many politicians, for example, are unknowingly serving the needs of the Negative Hierarchy. All dictatorships, whether religious or political, are agents for the materialistic powers. Evolution requires us to move our focus away from this physical world, so while people are focussed only on the physical world, the whole human evolutionary current is blocked. In fact, we are quite a bit behind our normal evolutionary scheme.

What we're trying to tell you is, there is a danger that more and more people will fall asleep because they have more material comforts, more gadgets to play with, and will completely forget that anything other than the material body and the material world exists. People will think they are having a fine life, except that when they go to the other side they will realize that they missed out on ninety-nine percent of life. But then it will be too late.

Why it is easy for the Negative Powers to act on human beings is because of *conditioning*, what we call tradition and culture. Every country has its tradition: how to behave, how to speak and how to act. Every religion has its tradition, and science, art, education and governments are preconditioned or cultured. In other words, a field of knowledge is memorized, repeated and then handed down from generation to generation, without anyone questioning it. For example, all the major religions have gone wrong. Buddhism, Christianity, Judaism and Islam have strayed from their original pattern, and nobody questions it. People do not realize that in all the ancient traditions many mistakes have crept in over the centuries, and they unconsciously accept and act on them.

This is precisely why the Negative Powers can keep our consciousness in the material world. Very few people dare to question the authorities. Those who dare question the established structure are of the New Age; the others are back in the Dark Age. And that, unfortunately, is the major problem that faces the Spiritual Hierarchy and those who are enlightened: How can the materialistic consciousness be moved so that people can think for themselves and ask, "Is that really so?" "Do we have to do that?" "Is that really what God wants us to do?"

This is just part of the battle going on at the moment for the planet, and for the Soul of Humanity. The Dark Forces will make it very easy, because the more comfort people have on the physical level, the more they do not care about spiritual things. That's why the mainstream religions have been losing millions of followers: as their standard of living gets better, people are not interested even in orthodox religion anymore. This is a real danger point. The next few hundred years will be a battle for the Soul of Humanity, so people will need *real* knowledge, *real* answers to questions like who are we? why are we here? and what do we have to do?

The New Earth

The next ten points are about the New Earth, which is about how all the events in the inner dimensions (the New Heaven) will work out practically in the Physical World, and how they will affect different aspects and departments of life.

Remember, these ten points are about how things *can* work out, depending on Humanity. A prophet sees energy-patterns, how energies work and what happens when they hit the Earth, but no prophet can tell how Humanity will react to them. How the cosmic situations are resolved depends on the intelligence, or lack of intelligence, of Humanity. If we handle the energies correctly, then there will be a Golden Age on Earth. If we do not handle the energies correctly, there will be a Dark Age. It's very simple, for there are only two choices: either we move forward or we stagnate and go backwards.

1. *Science*

We'll begin with science, which is one of the causes of the absolute domination of materialism over Humanity. In the seventeenth century, science established itself separately from the Roman Catholic Church, which up to then had ruled over every department of life, and now we have a science that has completely separated itself from anything that is of a spiritual nature. Science is basically mechanistic, like it was in the seventeenth century, and scientists think there is no intelligence behind Creation—no Soul, no Spirit, no God, no Transcendental Reality, no nonhuman reality—just physical, materialistic, mechanical explanations for everything.

When science recognizes that there is intelligence in *things*—intelligence in the atom, the planet, the Cosmos—then there will be a major breakthrough and science can *really* be useful to us. While it only has mechanical explanations for everything, science hinders the evolution of the planet. There is the One Universal Life pervading all, and every aspect of that Life has a meaning in the Cosmos. You cannot destroy one aspect without destroying another. If the scientists in Switzerland damage the atomic structure with their Large Hadron Collider, as I described previously, the disaster will be absolute and irreversible.

Another area of concern that falls under science is climate change and natural disasters. Scientists seem to think that human activities are the sole cause of climate changes and natural disasters, but these actually come from Mother Earth herself.

First of all, our Mother Earth is undergoing a cosmic expansion, a *cosmic initiation*, as part of her evolution, because the Solar Logos, the Sun, the ruler of the Solar System, is also undergoing a cosmic initiation. The Sun receives a tremendous, high-frequency energy from a more highly evolved Sun—in our case, the Central Spiritual Sun—who is in control of several Solar Systems and sends out tremendous waves of energy and new impulses into the Solar Systems, which then have to absorb them. Our Solar Logos transforms that energy to make it available to the planets within the Solar System. When this new energy hits our planet, the Earth struggles with it because it is a high-frequency energy and because an initiation is a stretching process, just as you get stretched when you get an initiation and seriously work with its energy-field. The whole idea of Initiation is to give you a new energy impulse, to create a new reality inside you, to make you develop along a new line—in a word, to stretch you.

Now, this planetary initiation takes centuries. The initiatory energy bombarding the planet Earth will have a strong impact for about five hundred years, and after that it will slowly equalize and stabilize within one thousand years from now. This means that there will be many earthquakes, extreme weather and natural disasters in the next few hundred years, all because the planet is trying to adjust its aura, its energy-field, to the new energies. When the Initiation process is over, the planet will settle down to a routine, normal way of living that will become available at that time.

So we don't have to blame Humanity for every disaster on this planet. Of course, we do add pollution, and that can be dealt with intelligently, but pollution is not what causes these vast cosmic happenings. We have to accept that there are going to be many natural disasters.

We should therefore think of our Mother Earth, instead of being selfish and thinking only of our own suffering. We are part of a cosmic living organism, atoms in the body of Mother Earth, but we can help her—which is the whole point! The human species is the *key* to the whole planetary development because the Human Hierarchy is the *guardian* of this planet. The angels cannot do it because they can work only in the inner dimensions, and of course the Animal Kingdom and the Plant Kingdom cannot look after the planet. The only species that can do it is the human species. If we apply our knowledge intelligently and live together harmoniously—instead of constantly waging wars!—we will help Mother Earth harmonize herself.

2. *Psychology*

At the moment, psychology is also materialistically based. Do not forget that the early psychologists were medical doctors who believed that the physical body and the physical world were the only reality, that the mind was the brain and that one's relationship to the outer environment was all that mattered. But in the next two or three hundred years psychology will also change along with science. The big breakthrough will come when psychology sees that a human being is a Living Soul, a ray of the Almighty Spirit, and that how human beings respond to the outer world is determined by their inner condition, how their Soul is functioning within. In other words, rather than looking at human behaviour outwardly as they do today, psychologists will go inside, in meditation, and find out what is the motive energy or force within the person that causes a particular problem or symptom.

There is always an internal motive energy that originates in a malfunction on the Soul level. The point is that human Souls are evolving—everything in the Cosmos is evolving—and because of that they have problems and imperfections that bring out certain characteristics in the personality. Violence, anger or whatever imperfections the human personalities have exist because the Soul cannot handle the material world. The Soul lives in the Causal World, which is a beautiful, harmonious world, but the Soul cannot control the energies here in the physical dimension and therefore there are the endless personality problems. When psychologists realize that the important thing is the *inner*, the Soul, how it expresses cosmic energies, how it expresses the drama of life, how it is limited in relationship to this outer world, then we will have *esoteric psychology*.

The word *psychology* is Greek, *psychē-logia*, which means the "science of the Soul", because in olden times in the Greek Mystery Schools, psychology *was* the science of the Soul. It was known that the Primary Man is the Soul, and the Soul has a mind, emotions and a physical body. The physical body was considered the outermost covering of the Soul, not the central figure as it is today. The central figure was the Soul and what was important was what the Soul did in relation to the mind, emotions and the physical body. At the moment, science and psychology deal with outer results, which are considered the causes of things. They are not. This is where psychology has to move more deeply inward and acknowledge the Soul and understand how the Soul tries to function in this physical world (which is a challenge for the Soul).

Don't forget that you *are* a Living Soul. When you exist as a Soul disjoined from your physical body, mind and emotions, you have the sensation of total freedom, of being everywhere and of being in perfect harmony with all things, being one with all things. When the Soul incarnates into the mental, astral and physical bodies, it is immediately crushed in, limited and hindered. How is it going to deal with that limitation? This is where the problems come in and this is where you need esoteric psychology to tell you that when you as a free entity (the Soul) get embodied into these limiting conditions (the personality), you react to these limitations and that's why you are as you are. Human psychology has to be explained from the inner point of view and then people will understand and change.

3. *Education*

Education has improved slightly since the seventeenth century but not in its basic idea, which still is to cram all kinds of information into the brains of students. That's not real education but at the moment it's considered education. In the future, education will be radically different; it will be Soul-oriented, like science and psychology, and the three will work together, recognizing that there is an Intelligent Principle in the human being and in the Cosmos.

Then education will be about how to develop inner intelligence through techniques of meditation, Sound-work, Light-work and all kinds of esoteric knowledge, and how to awaken the Soul to be more effective and take control of the personality's life circumstances. Education will be based on the fact that people are Living Souls embodied in this Creation, and it will be concerned with what is the best way for them to evolve and make themselves better.

That will be true education. It won't simply be memorizing facts and figures—the longest river, the smallest tree, the tallest building and all kinds of useless information. It will be about how to deal with the world and find one's purpose in life. There are a few educators, like Rudolph Steiner and Maria Montessori, who have already had the idea that education should be more than just memorizing anything and everything. When you go to school in the future, you are not going to memorize facts; instead, the teacher will ask you: "Who are you? What are you? Why are you here? What is your plan? What is your purpose?" The teacher will help you along those lines because he or she will also be an esoteric teacher, a knower of the inner realities.

4. *Religion—Piscean Devotion and Aquarian Mind*

At the moment, religion is what it was during the past 2,160 years of the Piscean Age, when the main keynote of religion was *devotion*. If you study the Hindu, Jewish, Muslim and Buddhist religious systems, you know that they are based on devotion. (The Buddhists do not believe in God but they believe in, and are devoted to, the Buddha, which is the same thing.) Therefore, all the techniques of meditation, chanting and rituals in religions were devotion-based.

At present, the Piscean energies are commingling with the new Aquarian energies because they have yet to die out. They will have an effect for another 150 to 300 years, during which time they will gradually weaken as the Aquarian energies increase. When the Aquarian influence is complete in one thousand years' time, religion will be all *mind*, no devotion.

This means that when people gather together in religious worship, they will use mental formulas. For example, people will visualize a geometric shape or some mental formula that they understand esoterically, and through that visualization the energy will come into them; no devotion will be required. Because we are in a transitory stage at present, it would be difficult for people to come together, visualize a mental formula and then go home and be happy with it. They need devotional stimulation because the Piscean energy is still strong. The problem is that many of the Aquarian esoteric groups, especially in the West, are mentally oriented, with no devotion in them whatsoever. That may be of the future, but it's not correct at the moment. The correct method is to link the Head Chakra, the Heart Chakra and the Base Chakra—to have knowledge of how things are, devotion to the supernatural realities and service to help Humanity realize the objective of the planetary goal.

5. *Death and Dying*

Because we live in a materialistic age, people think that the physical body is the only reality and when you die that's the end of the body, and the end of everything. That's why people are afraid of death. The only people who are not afraid of death are those who have had an out-of-body experience or a psychic, mystical or transcendental experience. They know that the physical body is a temporary house they live in, and when they die they will be in another world, an infinitely brighter and better world, so they are not afraid of death. But the one hundred percent materialists are afraid of death and hundreds of millions of people believe that when they die they are gone forever. But that will change, and I will tell you why.

Because of the energy spiralling down from the Inner Worlds that I mentioned earlier, people will begin to feel that they are immortal. The feeling of being another entity beyond the body, mind and emotions will become stronger and stronger in the next two or three hundred years until that downpour of energy will be so strong that people will automatically know that they are immortal beings living in many dimensions. They won't be afraid of death because they will know that when they die they just move from one dimension, one world, to another.[9]

This will be another radical change but, again, it will be a gradual one. Increasingly more people will have out-of-body experiences, near-death experiences, mystical experiences, occult experiences—all kinds of experiences that will prove to them that they are intelligent entities who can think and feel without a physical body. After a while society will naturally accept this. It won't be a big deal. When it's your time to go, you go; when it's your time to be born, you're born. It will just be part of the whole mechanism of Life.

6. *The Economy and Business*

The whole business world will also change. Now it operates on the idea of selfishness, getting what you can for yourself, making a profit for yourself—which is just a materialistic idea. This is why you read about big companies restructuring and dismissing half of their staff or cutting wages to make more profit for management and shareholders. They are motivated by selfishness.

Remember that making a profit isn't a bad idea in the early stages because one needs a motive power to succeed. If you talk to any businessman you'll find they are really keen about what they are doing, they are motivated, because they will have some profit or benefit. Otherwise, why would they bother? So businessmen work very hard. (If spiritual students would only work half as much they would be

9. See "The Secret of Death" on page 195.

Buddhas and Christs!) I've been in many train stations and airports, and everywhere I see businessmen on their computers or talking on their cell phones; wherever they are, they are doing their business with immense concentration.

As time goes on, however, business people will realize that making a profit only for yourself is not the ideal: you need to make a profit for everyone, to improve the life of everybody. There are already a few enlightened businessmen who think that business and the economy should benefit everybody, equally and holistically. This idea will gradually permeate the way business is done, so that rather than downsizing, companies will try to employ more people, to include more people in the growth and development process. Why? Because we are all one—one human family, one planet. As the other parts of society change, business practices will change and then there will be a completely new way of doing things.

7. Art

At the moment, art is still materialistic, although there are a few inspired artists trying to express something with a more spiritual meaning. Modern artists do whatever crazy thing they want to and call it art. I could give you many examples but one of my favourites occurred in London not too long ago. A young art student broke the window of a bus, jumped out and ran off. When people caught up with him and asked him why he did it, he said it was his thesis for art school. That's why I say that modern artists are confused about the idea of art; to them any action is art.

In the future, art will be based on beauty, truth and goodness. Then the whole way of creating art will change: it will be spiritually oriented. An artist will think of an idea that has to do with beauty, truth, goodness or harmony, then try to put it into a physical form or shape, whether it's painting, music, dance or some other form of art.

Nowadays art can be horrible. Why? Because the so-called artists are not in tune with higher realities; they are in tune with the material world. Look at the rap singers: they use very aggressive and violent language full of sexual and materialistic references. In other words, they are the very embodiment of the three lower chakras: the Base, Sex, and Solar Plexus Chakras. And they call that art. It is a *degeneration* of art. The future art will stimulate the mind and the heart and real artists will not make sounds and forms that are based on the lower chakras but on the upper part of the human system: the Crown, Third-Eye, Throat and Heart Chakras. It will be beautiful art.

8. *The Purpose of Life*

Many modern novels and movies, and modern philosophies, portray life as meaningless. They are highly intellectual and deal with all kinds of problems, but in the end they leave you with nothing: life is purposeless; there's nothing to it; it just happens. For example, a survey of thousands of people asking them what kind of books they read discovered an amazing thing: only four percent of people read spiritual books. To me, that is shocking news. It means that the intelligence of Humanity is such that most people are interested in fiction—not in reality, truth or what is real, but just something to amuse their minds. That's an incredible statement about the state of human consciousness regarding the purpose of life.

This will change. As the spiritual stimulation of the human family increases, many writers will write about ideas such as the Soul and Divine Intelligence as truths to live by. In other words, the whole purpose of life will be spiritual. As people are educated by Esoteric Knowledge and Esoteric Science about who we are and why we're here, materialism will change into true understanding, and more people will be interested in reading about spirituality, how things really are, instead of fiction, somebody's imagination of how things are.

9. *Health and Healing*

As you know, the medical profession treats illnesses by dispensing drugs to people. That is their solution to every disease, but there is a problem in that. Drugs are part of the Mineral Kingdom, so they reduce the vibration of the physical body to the level of the Mineral Kingdom; in other words, they make people dense and heavy and therefore further away from Soul impression. When you are on drugs you cannot register the Soul Light because the brain cannot register the light of the Soul unless it is bright, sharp and clear. When the brain is drugged, there is no way the Soul Light can even touch it.

The idea of getting people to consume large amounts of drugs is the work of the Dark Forces; they want to reduce people to the level of the Mineral Kingdom in functioning. Doctors, paid by the drug companies, prescribe drugs without understanding that they are helping the human species degenerate closer to the level of minerals, which is the most unintelligent part of Physical Creation. So, what's the solution?

In the future, doctors will realize that the human being is a body, mind and Soul, and that health problems are caused by factors other than physical ones, mostly etheric, emotional or mental causes in the energy-field around the body. Doctors will realize that a human being is a complex mechanism and it's not enough just to treat the physical body for health. They will look at the whole personality—the mind, emotions and etheric vitality of the person, which all influence the physical body. First they will ask if the Soul is in harmony with itself and its environment and next if the mind of the person is in harmony with itself and its environment. They will go through a whole gamut of causes to see how the illness manifested in the physical body. Only at the very end, when everything else fails, will they use what we call natural medicines, medicines that are nonharmful and part of Nature. The whole idea of healing will slowly change over the next few hundred years.

10. Politics

I want to deal with two major issues that could cause a major war—which is a *real* possibility.

(1) The Muslim World

If you study the history of the West you realize that from the second century onward the Roman Catholic Church dominated every aspect of people's lives. The Church persecuted anybody who was a free thinker, anybody who was motivated by progress, anybody who did not toe the line of the orthodox hierarchy. Because of this suppression by the Church, the Western World evolved to the idea of a government separate from the authority of the Church. So around the seventeenth century, people broke away and created separate governments. Once the state separated from the Church, people were able to think and there was an explosion of literature, art, science and new philosophies. The Western World developed all kinds of new ideas, including democracy and the equality of women.

The Muslim World missed that revolution. It didn't go through the Enlightenment or the Industrial Revolution that the European civilization went through over the last few hundred years. Muslim society was based on the Qur'ān, the Old Testament ways, and that's where it stayed. There was no progress of ideas like freedom of speech, freedom of thought or freedom of movement, no revolution separating church and state.

In the Muslim countries, the Church dominates every aspect of life and what's more it is back in the thirteenth century. Many Muslims do not understand democracy, religious freedom and freedom of thought. They are against those ideas, against the separation of religion from real life, and they resist new ways of doing things.

Also, Muslims have emigrated into European countries and to Australia, New Zealand, Canada, America and other countries. Many of them, unfortunately, want to keep the old ideas of the thirteenth century in their adopted countries. That could cause huge problems and there could be a clash between the Western World and the Muslim World. It has already started; it's been going on for decades now and it will increase. But remember, this is only a possibility. It can be avoided if those Muslims who want to enforce their outdated ideas change their ways and become democratic.

(2) China

The other big issue is China. For the past hundred years people have talked about what will happen when China awakes. Well, the so-called dragon has awakened: China has been increasing in power for decades. The Chinese do business in countries everywhere and they begin to have some control over them, because business is a big part of life. When China reaches its peak of development within the next ten to twenty years, it could be in position to build an empire because it is not only controlling countries economically, through business, but also increasing its army, navy and air force. China can spread its wings to many continents, so it could build a mighty empire which, when it is finished, would be the biggest in the history of the planet.

Ancient empires like the Persian Empire and the Roman Empire and modern ones like the Russian Empire under the communist system all lasted a certain number of years, but if China establishes an empire it could last for centuries. Why? Because the Chinese are united and well organized; they can plan ahead and maintain their plan. In the western democracies, everybody is for himself or herself. This is the failure of democratic countries: they do not understand group unity or group purpose at all. The Chinese understand the power of group unity. They can mobilize a billion people for the same objective, so they *can* conquer the world.

Besides China, there are smaller countries which are (or will become) dictatorships, usually under military control. In such countries, there is no freedom of choice in matters of religion or political decision-making, and their economic model is faulty. Dictatorships are based on the idea that we are all the same and we must all do and think the same way—and any other way is suppressed. Absolute dictatorship is always against change and progress, and it is usually the crystallization of an idea, sometimes even an idea that was originally a good intention. The free flow of ideas from the Spiritual Realms is essential to human progress and to the health of human beings. The Soul always seeks new ways for creative expression.

There is one more thing I want to say about politics. In every country there are problems between different nationalities that need to integrate. Every country has its own problems to deal with apart from problems with other countries. Whatever happens, however, depends on the intelligence of human beings and how they work out their problems. Human destiny is not a haphazard thing, not something uncontrolled or uncontrollable. It is exactly what human beings make it. That's all! If we make a mess of it, well, that's our destiny. If we react correctly, then we will have a Golden Age.

There *is* a way to peace. Howsoever the world is functioning, or not functioning, for each person there is a way to peace. The way is to *centre in your Soul.* The whole world can be totally chaotic, but if you are centred in your Soul you are at peace. The Soul is like a rock, an island in the ocean of the world with all its messy waves. Whatever happens in the future, you have one stable reference point and that is your Soul. The Soul survives everything; no problems of the world can reach it. If you establish yourself in Soul-Consciousness, you will be able to handle whatever happens.

On a larger scale, the more human beings that establish themselves in the Soul, the more peaceful the planet will become, and all these troubles will disappear. Human beings are so materialistic, so spiritually ignorant that they allow all the energies that come from the Cosmos to affect them in a negative way. Don't forget that the energies bombarding the planet are in themselves positive; it's only the human reaction that is negative. There are no wrong energies in the Cosmos, but wrong human reaction results in all the problems. While human beings are in a state of spiritual ignorance, bad things will happen. So my message is simple: Establish yourself in the Soul, be at peace and radiate that peace to all living things.

PART II

The Way of Light

The Development of Consciousness

If you ask people, what is consciousness? you will find that not many people actually bother to think about it at all. People think of sports, work, parties and what the government is doing or not doing, but who thinks about consciousness? Actually, consciousness is *the* thing; it's what makes you what you are.

First of all, it is a fact of life that we are all conscious, but how conscious we are, to what degree, is what determines who and what we are. In fact, it is the foundation of all life.

A stone is conscious. If you have cosmic sensitivity, you can tune into a stone and feel exactly what that stone is and what its consciousness is; you can look at a flower and discover the consciousness within the flower. Look at natural life: fish are conscious, birds are conscious, every living thing is conscious—an animal, a human, an angel, an archangel, a god, a Planetary Logos (the Spirit of a planet), a Solar Logos (the Spirit of a whole solar system) and so on. From the atom to the largest galaxy everything is conscious, and everything expresses a consciousness corresponding to its level of evolution, its own particular level of development.

Naturally, we can identify with the human level of consciousness, but not completely. We kind of know by our own experience what another human being is like and what sort of consciousness they have, but within the Human Kingdom the levels of consciousness are vastly different. Because of that it creates different societies: a simple consciousness produces a simple society while a complex consciousness produces a complex society. If you look at so-called primitive societies, their consciousness is usually centred on food—hunting, fishing, gathering—and simple manual tasks. Their level of consciousness is much simpler than that of societies in first-world countries. Gadgets like smart phones were not invented by simple people, but by developed, highly conscious people. The tools you work with show the level of your development.

This is important to know because here is the catch: you can actually develop consciousness. In other words, consciousness doesn't have to be static. Evolution, at the level of the human being, means that human beings have a choice to remain as they were born, in the society, culture, family they were born into, or to move beyond that. This is what we call the *Development of Consciousness*.

People just assume that consciousness exists, that everybody is conscious and that's it; there is no more to it and you don't have to do anything about it. But if you don't do anything about it you remain the same, at the particular level of development you have reached, and nothing more. And that's fine, if that's what you want to do. But what if you are not satisfied with that? What if you feel that there is something more to life? Then you have to do something about it—and that is: *change your consciousness*.

Whether it is applied to an individual person, a family, a community, a society or a whole nation, the principle is the same: If you want to change yourself, you have to change your consciousness. If you want to change your consciousness, you have to *do* something about it.

Nature doesn't force you to become something else. Nature has brought the human species to a certain level of development, but that is where Nature's job is finished. We are human beings. Now, if you want to move onto the level of the Angelic Kingdom, for example, you have to do something about your consciousness. In the same way, if the angels want to move to a higher level, to the Kingdom of the Gods, the angels have to do something about *their* consciousness. To move from point A to point B, every living species has to do something about it *consciously*, using their native intelligence, which is their consciousness.

Consciousness is not given to you as a gift; it has always been developed. For instance, the animals have a particular way of doing things because of the consciousness they developed over aeons of time. A cat behaves exactly as a cat should and a dog behaves exactly as a dog should, not because somebody told them to. No, they brought their behaviour with them in their consciousness. If they want to evolve from that level they have to consciously do something else, over and over again, until a new layer of consciousness develops over the old one. And it is exactly the same for human beings. If you want to change you have to understand where your consciousness is at, and then you have to do practical work over and over again until a new layer of consciousness dawns inside you.

For those who want to change their consciousness on the physical level only, there is worldly education. With education you can get a better job, learn about new things in life, expand your horizons and do many things that an uneducated person cannot do. That is changing your consciousness in this physical world, and that in itself is good; you will have better opportunities in this lifetime. But if you want to go beyond that, education has to be applied "vertically", in other words, internally or spiritually.

A normal worldly education is horizontal; a vertical education is one in which you learn about spiritual laws, how the Cosmos functions and how you as a Living Soul function in the Cosmos. Then you apply the practical techniques of meditation and spiritual exercises so that you can change the consciousness you were born with to another, higher consciousness. *That* is the Way of the Spiritual Path. Whether you follow the Warrior Path, or the Path of Yoga, Mysticism, Zen, Buddhism or other Spiritual Path, the process is the same. You have a vision of the goal ahead of you, understand what it takes to get there and start doing the practical work, systematically, over and over again until the old consciousness is overlapped with the new one.

There is a time lag between the old and the new consciousness, a stage of development that can be short or long depending on your aptitude, because it does not happen that you are conscious one minute and in the next you are superconscious. It doesn't work that way, unless you did the preliminary work in a previous lifetime and have brought over that ability. Some people attain a higher level of consciousness when they are teenagers and some are born with that consciousness. They have mystical experiences at an early stage of their lives; they know definitely what they have to do in this lifetime and they do it. *But they worked for it previously.* Even as children, that consciousness is operating inside them to free them from the prison house of the body, the prison house of the mind, the prison house of the environment, the family, the community, the nation, the world—of life itself.

That's why people talk about Enlightenment, Self-Realization or God-Realization, and why some people do it suddenly or do it over a long period of time, or never do it. It depends on their previous level of consciousness. If in your previous lifetimes you had mystical insights or inner experiences, naturally when you start thinking again about spiritual work, you regain the previous experience rapidly. If in the past you did nothing spiritual, just lived an average material life, then you are born with that level of consciousness and you have to start working intelligently day in and day out, year in and year out, until a new layer of consciousness becomes possible inside you.

It's the same as going, or not going, to school. If you do not go to school you have a certain level of consciousness as a natural human being—you will always have that because you are a member of the human species—but that's where it stays. When you go to school your consciousness changes through learning and schoolwork. When you go to university the input is larger and that changes your consciousness again. When you go to a spiritual school and apply spiritual meditation techniques, your consciousness changes even more so.

Consciousness and Spiritual Evolution

It is important to keep working to develop your consciousness because the Law of Consciousness states that you cannot be anything other than what your consciousness is. Where is your consciousness? That's where you are. If you are a religious person, you believe in Heaven or Hell or some kind of an afterlife, but it is only a belief system. In reality, the Law of Consciousness also applies in the after-death condition. Whether in this world or the next or the worlds after that, you can only be what your consciousness is. If you don't develop your consciousness before you die, you go exactly the same way as all the other people who did not develop their consciousness. The after-death conditions obey the same laws as life obeys. The Law of Consciousness applies in *all* places and at *all* times. Therefore you must work on your consciousness in this lifetime, in the here and now. Not only will it alter your life here but it will also alter your life in the after-death condition.

Consciousness is not your mind. Consciousness is not your emotions. Consciousness is not your body. Consciousness is a kind of permanent principle inside you that always was and always will be, but that permanent principle can contract or expand. It contracts when you are in incarnation. Why? Because it attaches itself to your mind, emotions and physical body, becoming limited and contracted by assuming those forms. Consciousness uses those forms, or rather limits itself by those very forms, but it has to use them to be able to function in this world.

Before incarnation you are a limitless being, but you have to have a body to do things in this world; you have to have emotions to *feel* so that you are able to tune into other people and other things; and you have to have a mind to think, to reason, to understand and to remember things. These are instruments Consciousness uses so that you can function as a normal human being in a normal human world, and they are all good. When you understand this, you say to yourself, "I am a limitless being and have come down and contracted myself into this limited self, the human personality, so now I am going to reverse the process and expand myself to the limitless horizons I came from."

This expansion happens to some extent when you die a natural death. When you die you drop your physical body and your consciousness immediately enlarges because the physical body is not hampering it any more. You still have your emotional nature (and mind-structure), but because you have no physical body your consciousness is larger since your emotional nature in the other world, the Astral World, is much vaster than in the Physical World. Already in the after-death condition you feel much more alive, bright and conscious. When you die in your astral body, you drop your emotional nature and you go to the Heaven Worlds, which are dimensions of the Mental World, and then your consciousness expands again by nature, because it is not hindered by emotional factors. When you die in your mental body and drop your mind-structure altogether your consciousness is completely bright and open again, almost as it was in its original state, because even the subtle mental vibrations of the Heaven Worlds no longer influence your consciousness. This is what we call Soul-Consciousness, consciousness of yourself as a Soul living in your causal body. Now when you drop your causal body and move beyond the Causal Mind, the subtlest form of mental activity, you are awake in a bright Sea of Consciousness.

The lesson to be learned is that as human beings we have a choice in this lifetime. We have a choice to remain exactly as we are or we can consciously want to be more real, to have more consciousness, to see the bright side of Life. Once you have decided that you want to be more than what you were born with, of course you have to start working, using forms of meditation and spiritual techniques that enable your consciousness to escape its limitations. It is not that meditation does anything *for* you; it never does. What it does is enable your consciousness to escape its limitations. In our personality, consciousness is very restricted. But once you learn certain techniques you can move out of that limitation and have glimpses or experiences of the more extended states of being. That being is your nature; it's not something given to you from the outside, not something you can buy in a shop. It's what you already are when you free yourself from limitations.

There are two ways whereby we can liberate our consciousness: the Way of Activity and the Way of Passivity. Both are equally important; using only one or the other will result in imbalance. If you only use the techniques of Passivity you will quit this world and you will no longer be consciously active in the world. This is what yogis in India or people who renounce the world do. They shut the outer part of Reality out of their consciousness and concentrate on the inner part of Reality so that they can expand their consciousness in the Inner Worlds. That's fine, but then they are no longer able to fulfil their destiny in *this* world.

In Switzerland, for example, people are educated and have a high standard of living, a good *material* life, but that's where it stops; there is no spiritual education. In India, on the other hand, people do not have much material education, there is poverty and misery, but they have spiritual education because they believe in spiritual realities. They chant, meditate and do many religious activities, but they have neglected material education. On the spiritual level there is a high-frequency vibration; on the material level there is absolute chaos. These are examples of unbalanced conditions.

Our way is balanced. Through the Way of Activity, or the Way of Action, we work out our karma and do the right thing for society and for the human species. Through the Way of Passivity, or the Way of Calmness, we increase our connection with the inner dimensions, the inner realities, and thereby expand our consciousness to ever-vaster horizons. We do both at the same time in our school in order to create perfect human beings.

A perfect human being is somebody who is able to give society what society needs and at the same time give the Soul what the Soul needs. Otherwise you are at one extreme or the other, and neither extreme is any good. If you concentrate on activity and become one of those who are always doing something, you cannot move away from your level of evolution at that stage. Even if you are the most charitable person and spend a lot of your time doing charity work in developing countries, your consciousness remains exactly the same. The Way of Activity still gives your consciousness the same boundaries and limitations that existed before you started. You need the other way, the Way of Passivity, to stretch your consciousness into the Unknown, into the Infinite. You need to have both the horizontal (outer) life and the vertical (inner) life simultaneously expressed. Then your life forms the Cross (vertical and horizontal) and you are a perfect human being in society and fulfil your destiny as a member of the human species.

Ultimately, if you reach a high level of consciousness, it will liberate you altogether from the *necessity* to be born as a human being. At this stage we are so identified with the human structure that we can't imagine being anything other than a human being. People are suspicious of the idea that you can change yourself from a human to an angel, from an angel to a god and from a god to a super-god. Why? Because they only identify with their human nature; they can't identify with something greater than that. If you move along the Spiritual Path you will become greater than your ordinary human nature; you will become superhuman. This is precisely what Spiritual Evolution is about. You have to go beyond the species that you are to a higher species, and from that to another higher species, and from that to yet another higher species. That is what we call Cosmic Evolution.

The same is possible for everybody, even people who have never thought of it before, if they know that they have to educate themselves—physically to get a better job and better life, and spiritually to have a better evolutionary level of being. And everyone can get there, because that is another law. The Law of Consciousness is such that Consciousness is self-developing; it feeds itself. Once you light a fire and keep feeding it with wood, the fire will keep going. If you want to change your consciousness you have to feed it with more consciousness, or with exercises that feed consciousness so that it grows. And as your consciousness grows you have glimpses of other realities that are possible for it.

There are five points I want to tell you about Consciousness and how to develop it.

1. Consciousness evolves.

Many human beings are happy just to be as they are; they are happy just to have the same consciousness as their parents, religion or culture. Well, there's nothing wrong with that; it just means that their consciousness is not evolving, just staying at the same level at which they started. People become crystallized in their religion, their tradition, their politics, their science, their art. Which means they are stuck.

But Consciousness evolves. This means that as you are, you are not perfect. Something inside you that is conscious, the real being inside you, wants to move on toward perfection. It is an inborn part of human nature that we want to become more, greater, larger and experience more of life. This is why many people at a certain time in their life will feel an inward urge to change, to be more than what they were born with, more than what their environment gave them. This is a sign that their consciousness is evolving.

So you don't have to be static; you can move ahead (and you must move ahead) once that stirring happens inside you. It can happen in a thousand different ways: you may come across a book, a person, an idea, any number of things that push you along toward your objective on the Spiritual Path.

So the first important lesson to understand is that Consciousness evolves, and once you are ready it will move you along.

2. ***The mind reacts to what is seen, heard, felt, smelled or tasted (the senses).***

The physical body has the ability to see, hear, feel, smell and taste, and every time you get an impression of the outside world through the physical body, your mind reacts to it, automatically and instantaneously. You don't have to think about it; it just happens. And that is precisely the problem.

For example, let's say you are trying to meditate and a thought comes into your mind because you remembered some sensory experience of heat or cold, pain or pleasure, good or bad or whatever. That disrupts your meditation. There are millions of distractions: you may hear the telephone ringing or the kids making noise; sensations come in from the outside world and you immediately react to them. Or even just the *memory* of a sensation from the outside world—anything from the past—may pop up. It is not only the immediate environment that you react to but also memories of whatever sensations you saw, felt or heard.

Somehow, all this mental activity has to be overcome if you want to attain spiritual states of Consciousness. It is the function of the senses to convey information to the mind about the world around you, and it is the function of the mind to assess them, which under normal conditions is perfectly valid and how it should be. But it's different when you try to meditate. When you try to meditate it becomes a problem.

So know firstly that you can move ahead in Consciousness and secondly that the mind is an obstruction that is always there for you as a challenge.

3. ***For Consciousness to evolve, there must be a way to control the modifications of the mind. Otherwise you remain forever the same.***

The people who devised meditation techniques understood that if you want to move ahead in Consciousness you have to do something with all the stuff that the mind reacts to. For your consciousness to evolve, in other words, you must have a way to control the modifications the mind goes through while you are meditating so that you can move to a higher layer of Consciousness, a higher level of experience of Reality. We are talking about meditation only; we don't mean that you should walk around like a zombie all day trying to control your mind. There must be a way to control the mind during the time of meditation.

There are hundreds of millions of people all over the world who remain the same. They react to whatever the senses tell their mind, and that's it. They don't actually make any movement in life whatsoever. They are born with a certain frequency of vibration and they die with that same frequency of vibration, because they do not learn to control those modifications, which go on automatically. We call that the *state of sleep*. Their consciousness is sleeping; it is not stirring and they are not doing anything about it.

Those of you who have read books on meditation know that there are many ideas about meditation, thousands of books from all religions and all traditions telling you how to meditate. The majority of them, however, are completely wrong; they do not have the right purpose. They try to make you rich, to give you influence over people, to help you relax or make you "happy" on the personality level. There is nothing wrong with trying to improve your personality or become more capable in a particular part of your life. But it's not the true purpose of meditation. You can work hard and do all the things necessary to be rich and famous, but that is not going to get you a divine state of Consciousness.

The purpose of meditation is not to attain worldly glory but spiritual glory, the perfect state a human being should be, what a human being was originally intended to be. We have a higher view of meditation and therefore our way must be different. We must still practise to control the modifications of the mind, as everybody has to regardless of their purpose, but our objective is very different. We have the highest vision in view, the great archetypal plan for Humanity, what the human being needs to do to become perfected in a particular lifetime. We work for that and nothing less.

4. *Your consciousness and your body are not the same ...*

We mentioned earlier that through the senses you receive impressions and then your mind reacts to them. In the normal systems of meditation and in the normal thinking of the world, your consciousness and your body are the same, therefore whatever impressions you receive through your body constitute what you do, what you are and what you become. But here is where we make a huge distinction; we say your consciousness and your body are *not* the same.

Your body does what it's supposed to do. It conveys sensations to the mind and the mind reacts to them. Most people think that that is their consciousness. When they see a tree, their eyes convey the message to the mind and the mind says it's a tree, and that's the end of it. But we say that there is something more profound at work in a human being: a possibility for supernatural or higher evolution beyond that of normal human evolution.

Your consciousness is formless, bodiless and pure—and independent of physical life.

If you have what is called an out-of-body experience or near-death experience you will discover that your consciousness is not your body, that it exists outside of your body. There are many people in the world who have experienced this. It's still only a psychic experience and not the same as, say, SAMĀDHI (Spiritual Ecstasy), but it is a step in the right direction. It's quite normal to identify yourself as something other than your physical body. When you die, for instance, that is exactly what you experience. You leave your body behind and you start living in the Astral World. You go and visit your relatives and do whatever. (You may get angry at the people who are mourning and crying at your funeral because you are getting their negative vibrations, which are spoiling your fun.) The near-death and death experiences show you that you are different from your physical body.

Once you understand that your consciousness is formless, bodiless and pure and that it is independent from physical life, you begin to understand the real ways of reaching, through meditation, higher states of Consciousness, or the direct experience of Reality as it really is, not how it appears to be.

5. *Evolution is twofold: your body and your consciousness ...*

Science knows that there is such a thing as evolution but its idea of evolution is extraordinarily limited. It tries to trace how fish escaped the ocean and somehow started evolving on land, how on land there were dinosaurs and many strange creatures and how the human species evolved from monkeys. The scientific view is wrong—we did not evolve from monkeys—but the idea of evolution itself is right. There is evolution going on, but it is not only the physical body that evolves through natural processes; Consciousness evolves also. And this is the important thing. You are not simply a being who evolves through the physical body, but you have a separate reality—Consciousness—that is also evolving.

Now, Nature takes care of your physical body evolution; you don't have to interfere with it or do anything about it. But here is the point: so far as *Consciousness* is concerned, you must take care of the evolution of your consciousness yourself.

***You* are responsible for the development of *your* consciousness.**

You can forget your physical body in terms of evolution and just do what is required for its health and well-being. Nature takes care of itself. Mother Nature deals with the form side of life: the physical body, the physical world, physical creation. Nature takes care of all that but so far as *your* consciousness is concerned, you must take care of it yourself. Nature will not do it. You consciously have to decide that you will evolve in *this* lifetime, that you will attain Enlightenment, or a divine level of Consciousness. There is no other way. So you must work, work, work and work to develop your consciousness.

And there is another thing that is very important: service. Service is working selflessly for your Teacher, for your spiritual group and for the cause of enlightening Humanity about the spiritual way of life. Many people understand that they have to do something about their consciousness to become enlightened, but it is essentially a selfish purpose; they do it for themselves only. They can make some progress, yes, but unless they are oriented toward service they will not attain a perfect state. They will reach the stage of a PRATYEKA BUDDHA, one who is enlightened for himself or herself alone. This is a limited Enlightenment. The real Enlightenment is one that enables you to work for others. The power, glory, wisdom, understanding and love you develop through the process of Enlightenment, you give to others. Then you become a truly enlightened Buddha, a SAMYAKSAṀ BUDDHA.

As I mentioned previously, a transition period is needed between the old and new consciousness. This means that you do not become enlightened straight away unless you have developed that faculty in previous lifetimes. It may take a year, ten years, thirty years or more to reach Higher Consciousness; it depends totally on *you*, on how much work you did in the past and what your capacity is now and how much effort you are putting into it. To make a great accomplishment, whether it is in sports, art or whatever, you always have to practise hours and hours every day. Most people understand that. But when it comes to spiritual life they think that all they have to do is sit down and meditate, and that's it. This is a delusion because spiritual life is just as demanding as any form of art or athletics. You still have to put in the time.

The Crown Jewel of Knowledge

The Forces of Unification

This is important knowledge in terms of understanding the plan, purpose and destiny of your life and of the state of the world. It is esoteric knowledge that will help you deal with existence itself. Before you can work out your Salvation, you have to understand this existential reality:

The basic nature of Material Creation is Disintegration.

In this Universe nothing is permanent and nothing can be permanent. The very Material Creation is based on Disintegration. If something is born, it will have to die; if something grows, it will have to decline; everything that is put together falls apart. This is the Basic Law of Material Creation. Disintegration is inherent in existence itself.

By *Material Creation* we mean the Physical World, the Astral World and the Mental World. These three realms are what we call the perishable realms, which are always changing and renewing themselves through birth and death. *Everything* in Material Creation is always disintegrating, but that is not a negative thing; you have to look at it positively. If the Universe around us did not disintegrate we would be *stuck.* Imagine if we were back in the Dark Ages, when the Church ruled by terror and torture during the Inquisition. Imagine if that system had not disintegrated. The very fact of disintegration helps us move forward so that we don't get locked into one bad state, or even a good state; we don't get locked into one situation forever.

So, the Law of Disintegration is basic and positive, but it is only one part of the Law. The other part is:

In order to maintain yourself *and* to reach the Eternal, you need the Forces of Unification.

There are two things involved here. First, to maintain your physical body, emotional nature and mental nature and every aspect of your life (because everything is disintegrating all the time) you need to have something to balance the disintegration. That "something" is the Forces of Unification, which are energies and powers that work in reverse of Disintegration. Second, to reach the Eternal, the Timeless, the Transcendental, the Absolute, that which never changes—for that you also need the Forces of Unification.

This means that to maintain your life—your health, relationships, job, family, environment—you need the Forces of Unification because if they are not active in your life, everything in and around you automatically disintegrates. That's why families disintegrate, communities disintegrate, nations disintegrate, empires disintegrate. It's natural for that to happen, if people do not understand that there are forces that work in the opposite way, for Unification.

Besides maintaining yourself in your present embodiment, however, you need the Forces of Unification to reach *beyond* that, into the Eternal Reality That Never Changes. And this is where the lack of esoteric knowledge comes in. Many people try to reach the Eternal—or Nirvāṇa, Self-Realization, God-Realization, the Ultimate Truth or whatever you like to call it—but they do not understand that they are living in a universe that is always disintegrating, and that there are forces that *counter* this disintegration and must be used for one's Salvation. They do their best and then find they cannot concentrate, or other problems always crop up. Most of them never achieve their goal because they do not know that disintegration is normal, that it's how Nature works, but that there is another set of *unifying* forces that they can use.

Next, let us consider how this Unification process works, that is, which forces within you need to be unified. That is the key.

First of all, why you do not succeed, whether it is a spiritual quest or a material quest, is because your inner forces are continually causing disintegration. To understand this on a practical level, when you have an idea to do something, how quickly do you get sidetracked? As soon as you decide that you want to become a doctor, lawyer, dentist or the prime minister of New Zealand, disintegration starts immediately and things come up to prevent you from achieving your goal—*unless* you understand the Law and invoke the Forces of Unification to stop the disintegration and take you to your vision or goal. In other words, your inner forces need to be unified to succeed in this life in anything whatsoever, including your great quest for the Eternal.

So, what needs to be unified inside you?

(1) Your Physical Forces

If you want to be successful in anything, whether it is the Spiritual Path or passing an exam or in *any* situation whatsoever, one of the things you need to do is unify your physical forces. By *physical forces*, we mean the energy or the ability of your physical mechanism to do things. Even if you are studying for an exam you have to have your physical body in reasonably good shape. If you are staying out late every night and consuming large amounts of alcohol, when the examination time comes you will realize that you are not physically fit to take the exam. To be successful in any project you need your physical forces unified.

(2) Your Emotional Forces

Strange as it may seem, a lot of people are moody, upset, argumentative, angry or annoyed and think nothing of it; they think it's normal. For *any* success you must have your emotional forces under control, unified and singularly directed to one purpose. If your emotions are running wild you will never succeed even in the simplest thing; you will have problems straight away. Whatever you do, from the simplest to the greatest, your emotional forces *must* work in unison.

(3) Your Mental Forces (Thoughts)

Obviously, if your thoughts are all over the place and not focused on what you are doing, you will fail.

So with any project, from the simplest physical job to the ultimate project of reaching Enlightenment, you have to have your *physical* forces unified, your *emotional* forces unified and your *mental* forces unified in order to attain your goal. The disintegrating forces work automatically—you don't have to think about them or invoke them—so you must intelligently counter them by unifying your physical, emotional and mental forces.

Then you have what is called an *integrated personality*, which means that your body, emotions and mind function as a single unit, focused on your objective. All the energies of the personality are driving towards that objective and you will succeed, whether you are in the field of sports, politics or any creative field. If you have single-minded concentration and your internal physical and emotional energies are unified, you *will* succeed. That's the secret of success.

I'm sure you have met people in your life who you felt were integrated. They always know what they are doing and they do it. They have an energy around them that is positive, dynamic, active and successful.

All their forces on the personality level work together in unison. They may not know about the occult law but they do it automatically—for whatever reason. You do not have to know about the Law, but it's better if you do because then you can consciously use it yourself.

Integrating the Personality and the Soul

Becoming an integrated personality in this lifetime is the first stage. Then, in order to move into the next stage (reaching the great ideal of Enlightenment and becoming a Master Adept), your integrated personality must be united with your Soul, the Being of Light within you (the Being of Light that you *are*). I'm talking about when you are moving onto the Spiritual Path, when you are moving beyond worldly objectives. That is the next stage of development and it is only for those who want to do it, of course. The average man or woman in the world is not interested in connecting with their Soul, but if you want to you can do it through what we understand as the Spiritual Path, the vast field of spiritual practices like meditation, chanting, Sound work, exercises and other means by which the personality becomes united with the Soul.

How quickly you can integrate your personality with your Soul depends on many factors: your ability to concentrate, the vision you have of what you want to do, your strength of purpose, and so on. If you only have a weak idea of what you want to do and do not put much action towards it, you won't get there. There is no time frame for the personality to unite with the Soul, because it is different for everybody. For people making a little effort it will take longer; for people making an all-out effort it will be shorter. Time is an irrelevant factor; whatever success you have in the spiritual field is all about your effort. In any case, this is what must happen:

Your integrated personality must be united with your Soul using the Forces of Unification, and then you become a *Soul-infused personality*, a Master Adept.

What this means is that you are actually one hundred percent different from the normal human being. Why? Because the average person works on the personality level only. They may be the most successful business person, politician, artist, scientist or whatever, they may be integrated on the personality level, but they still have not linked up with the Soul, so they are ordinary. The ordinary people live in the personality dimension and the Master Adepts live in the Soul dimension. To them, the Soul dimension is reality and the personality dimension is only a shadow world. They live in the bright daytime of the Soul, not the dark nighttime of the personality. They are focused on Soul expression, how the Soul expresses itself in Time and Space, not on the personality expression.

In other words, as a Master Adept you are a completely different human being; you are one step ahead on the evolutionary line and you have entered the Spiritual Kingdom, or what the Christ called the Kingdom of God. You are still a personality but your point of view is radically different. Your attention is focused within and everything you do is motivated from within. It is difficult to understand unless you are born with this ability or have achieved it through hard work in this lifetime. Everything you do has a completely different effect than if you were just an ordinary, integrated personality. What comes out is the *power* of the Soul, the energy of Light that *knows* and *understands*. It is the Soul that assesses the situation and does the action, which is very different from when you, even as an integrated personality, assess a situation and act.

This explains why people who reach the stage of a Soul-infused personality, or Master Adept, always think differently, act differently and are different from ordinary people. Often they are misunderstood because people expect them to have the same points of view that they have, to be on a narrow track like they are and choose one idea or another. But Master Adepts see things from above, like an eagle looks down and sees the valley, the mountain and the valleys on the other side. They see the train going into the tunnel and then coming out the other side, whereas a normal person only sees the train disappear into the tunnel. Master Adepts have a large vision; their assessment is not based on the immediate circumstances. It is because of this large vision that they know what will be the right action.

Now, when you reach the state of the Master Adept that gives you the power to become the *master of your destiny*. That is the final result of the whole unification process inside you. Being the master of your destiny means that you see the past, future and present, and according to that vaster knowledge field, you make the right decision about what you should do in a particular situation. You can actually change a situation … to suit what? *Not yourself*, but the larger Reality. This is the other thing that is difficult to understand about Master Adepts: they don't think of themselves. When they do an action it is not because they want to get something out of it; it is because they see the wider circle of Reality, how one action would be better than another, how one action would impact more people in a more positive way.

In other words, their consciousness encompasses societies and nations and considers the *benefit* of the larger number of people. The most successful people on the personality level only consider what they deem good for themselves, how *they* benefit from a business deal or a political move. When the Masters think they don't consider what benefits them; their personality needs don't come into it. And that is why it is difficult to understand such people when they suggest a course of action, because most people would interpret it in terms of their own personal *want*. A Master Adept has no personal wants. They look and see what would be the best thing for the situation.

The Forces of Unification and the Forces of Light

We have considered the theme of the Forces of Unification in terms of the individual, and now we will look at it in terms of the wider picture, the world picture:

> **The planetary evolutionary forces are driving all things towards Unification, or Oneness.**

The idea that there are intelligent forces driving evolution may be a strange idea for some people who do not even know that there is such a thing as evolution. In school, evolution is taught as Charles Darwin's theory, which he formulated by studying animals and plants on small islands. But that is only a fragment of a fragment of Evolution, which is much, much vaster than that.

This is a highly esoteric subject by which you can gauge movements and situations on this planet, on a small or large scale, by seeing that there are two kinds of forces that are always active: the disintegrating forces and the integrating forces. The Forces of Disintegration are easy to see. You have a beautiful flower and in a few days' time it has died. But can you see the tremendous unifying forces working through the planet? This is an ability you have to develop: when you look at things, see what forces are acting on them—Disintegration or Unification—and acknowledge both. Only when you can acknowledge both can you know the right action; otherwise, you are always making the wrong choices.

The forces driving towards Unification work on different scales: the self, the family, the group, the nation, between nations and between continents.

From now on, when you listen to or watch the news or when you are dealing with people, try to pick up what side they are on: the destructive side or the unifying side. Start with yourself and consider whose side you are on. Look at your family, your group, your nation and the interaction between nations and even between continents. If you can see how these forces are acting on an ever-larger scale, you will have the right understanding and be able to make the right choices. If you want to be on the side of Evolution, for the greater good of all, then you must follow the Forces of Unification because *they are the Forces of Light.*

The important thing is to watch yourself, watch what is happening to you, and be sure you are always on the side of the Forces of Light, no matter what, even if you have to personally sacrifice yourself. Often people do sacrifice themselves. A good example is the Master Jesus, who sacrificed Himself for the people of Israel. He didn't have to do it; he chose to do it because he saw that through His personal sacrifice the people of Israel would reap a tremendous benefit at that time from the Forces of Light coming in. You can see that He was a great Soul-infused personality who worked as a Soul, not as a personally ambitious person.

The Forces of Light always follow Unification and Oneness. The Forces of Darkness always follow Disintegration and Separation.

We are presuming that you are at a stage of development where you take an interest in life, in what goes on around you and inside you, and you know that you have to make conscious, intelligent choices about things—between what suits you, the ego, and what suits the larger purpose. Following the Forces of Light is always the right thing to do.

The Forces of Light can only work one way: toward Unification. The Forces of Darkness can only work one way: toward Disintegration.

This is not a philosophy or theory; it is real and you can observe it around you all the time, everywhere. People who are on the side of Light always try to unify things, to make them one, make them benefit the whole community. Those who follow the Forces of Darkness are always selfish, separating themselves and wanting things only for themselves or for their little group.

We do not mean that human beings are purposefully doing that. If someone wants to disintegrate his group, it doesn't mean that he is consciously a black magician. It simply means that he is not able to discriminate between right and wrong, between the energies of Light and the energies of Darkness. He is not high enough on the ladder of evolution to be able to sense which is a positive energy and which is a negative energy.

What we're trying to say is that at the stage of human evolution reached on this planet at this time, the Forces of Darkness, the forces of disintegration and separation, are very strong. You can see this in any country, and unfortunately most human beings are under that influence. Why? Because they are not sensitive *internally*, they are not aware that there are two different forces at work.

When it comes to politics, principles, laws or actions to take, there are always two ways: uniting or disintegrating. If you are in a responsible position in your community or your country, you should always make decisions that lead to unification. When there is a decision to be made ask yourself one question: Is it separative or is it uniting? There is no in-between. You must always be on the side that unites, the side that is for the greater good; otherwise, you are following the Path of Darkness.

If you are a spiritual disciple, moreover, you must always follow the Path of Unification, even if it is a personal sacrifice. That is why the Christ said, "If you want to be my disciple, take up your cross and follow me" (*Matthew* 16: 24). "Follow me" means, of course, follow the Path of Unification, the Way of Oneness, and "take up your cross" means sacrifice, sacrificing yourself for the greater good of all.

And lastly:

> **Unification—within you or within the world—is achieved by action and effort. It does not happen by itself.**

This is important as a statement of your purpose of being a human being and your purpose of being a spiritual disciple. If you want to unify yourself, you have to make an effort towards it. If you want to unify your family, you have to make an effort towards it. If you want to unify your group, you have to make an effort towards it. If you want to unify your country, you have to make an effort towards it. In other words, unification needs human beings to bring it about; it does not come by a change in the weather or by itself. It involves *intelligence* and it needs to have people who can make a *conscious* effort.

As I said, sometimes you have to make a personal sacrifice for the sake of the larger good, to take up your cross and carry it, and sometimes to even be crucified, because you are becoming Soul-conscious. When you are conscious of your Soul, or rather your Soul is conscious of *you*, then your vision is large. You see the moment but, simultaneously, you also see the causes stretching back into the past and you see what is going to happen in the future. Then, in the balance of past and future, you know the right action. Sometimes you can do it quite easily, and sometimes you have to give up your life. It all depends on the circumstances. But the main thing is that you are doing your duty and acting as a *spiritual being* on this planet.

PRACTICE

~

A Spiritual Exercise for Group Unification

This meditation exercise uses ŌṀ, the word of Unification. First, the group intones the word ŌṀ physically, aloud, three times, using a bright, clear tone. Then the group intones it mentally, silently, using the same bright and clear sound. The sound of ŌṀ becomes a unifying energy-field whose subtle energies vibrating in the room will unite the group like never before.

Internally, each person intones ŌṀ in their own time, followed by a pause and then another intonation. In each pause, focus on the stillness as it slowly builds into a tremendous field of Silent Energy.

The Way of Happiness is the Way of Light

Most people want to be happy. And of course most people have no idea where to look for happiness. They usually look for happiness in money or in material things, thinking that those things will make them happy. But if you look at the lives of rich people you will see that they are not necessarily happy; they are often miserable. The poor are also miserable, and so are the in-betweens. It seems that being miserable is just a fact of life. The reason for this is simply that people are looking for happiness in the wrong places.

If you look for happiness *in the world* you will never find it. Of course, the great Saints and enlightened Sages and Teachers have been telling Mankind for the last ten thousand years not to look for happiness in the world, but people still do that. *Nothing of the world will give you happiness.* Full stop. So the question arises: If you can't be happy in the world, how can you be happy? The answer is: the Way of Happiness is the Way of Light.

Basically, everybody is unhappy because they do not have enough Light-Energy or Light-Vibration inside them. When you have Light inside you, you are happy, bubbling over with happiness. Happiness is actually how much Light-Energy is sparkling inside you. You can be completely uneducated, completely destitute and poor, but if you have Light inside you, you are full of joy and happiness. In other words, depression, anger, violence, negative feelings, bad moods, attachment to the miserable situations of life—they are all redeemed by the Light inside you. That Light can help you remain stable even amongst the worst worldly situations.

It is important to understand that the world *is* coming apart; it is changing rapidly and not necessarily in a happy direction. Increasingly, there are going to be struggles and problems in the world, and you need to have Light so that you are not affected by the coming changes. During the Second World War, and also during past and present dictatorships, whenever people were jailed or tortured because they were against the system, there were always some who managed to preserve their sanity because they had the Light inside them. I'm talking about a large amount of Light, when the Light is really functioning inside you, when the sheer, bright radiance of the Light is so overwhelming that it overcomes any negativity inside and outside you. Whatever happens in the world, you will be happy, because nothing can stop that all-conquering Light from bubbling like a fountain of joy inside you.

Light is the Soul Connection

The problem with people is that the Soul is not strong enough to control the personality; the Soul is not in command of the personality. So the idea is to connect the personality to the Soul. This connection has nothing to do with outer circumstances. You don't have to be successful in art, business, politics or science to connect with your Soul. Outer worldly success is relative; you can do it or not do it; it's your choice. But it has nothing to do with your Soul. *Nothing you do in the world has anything to do with your Soul.*

So what is this connection? It is Light. That's why you need to have more and more Light inside you, because only the Light can connect you to your Soul. Why? Because the Soul *is* Light (your Soul is made of pure Light) and only Light attracts Light.

The personality is made of matter. Now, matter is also Spirit—everything is Spirit—but matter is of a low-frequency vibration, much lower in vibration than your Soul. This is why people are not normally aware that they are Souls. Seven billion people are focused on the personality level, which is a materialistic energy-field of a certain vibration, but the Soul vibrates in a field of Light, and there's no connection between the two. You have to make a conscious, intelligent connection, you have to work and increase that connection, and then the personality will slowly diminish until only the connection with the Soul remains. Then you are on the Way of Light.

Then you really understand why the great Saints and Masters only talked about the connection to the Soul, not about personal development or how to get rich and famous. Why? Because the Soul lives in a world of Light, a world of absolute Joy, absolute Bliss, absolute Happiness, absolute Love—everything that you have ever wanted; there is nothing that you desire which is not in the world of the Soul.

The objective of our School is to link you up with your Soul (and beyond the Soul, with Ultimate Reality). It is not a school for personal development, to make you rich and famous in the world or to overcome personal problems (problems you produce with your own personality and then try to solve with the same personality that produced them in the first place). No, a school is only valid when it shakes you up, when it awakens you and makes you think: "Hey, this is it! *This* is what I want to do in life." Otherwise you might as well go to a university and learn about all kinds of philosophies so that you pass an exam. It doesn't do anything to you *internally*.

Now, the larger objective is not only for you to connect to your own Soul individually but also for humans to connect en masse to the Soul of Humanity. For the past six thousand years, in every country, East,

West, North and South, people worked for their own Salvation. It was normal to disconnect from the world and look for your Salvation by whatever means and knowledge you had. Buddha did it and the ancient Prophets of the East and West did it. But the situation has changed: we no longer seek Salvation only for ourselves but on a group basis and then beyond the group for Humanity, for the planetary life, the *planetary consciousness* itself. Our Esoteric School was established for that reason: to connect the individual personalities to their Souls and connect the group of personalities to the Group Soul, which then opens up enormous possibilities for Humanity.

To do this, a spiritual group has to attain a unified vision and understanding of what it is doing and to work together as one single Soul-Group. This means that all those who remain individualistic, who cannot stand the group-energy, the group-consciousness, will fall away. The Christ called this "the separation of the sheep and the goats" (*Matthew* 25: 32). And this process of separation is also happening on a large scale in the world; that is, the separation of those who can move into the New Reality because they have the Light inside them, and those who cannot. The brighter the Light inside you, the more chance you have to move into the New Reality, and those who have no Light will be left behind. This is the law of Life, the law of Nature.

The New Reality is about the Kingdom of God, which is in the process of appearing in the physical world. When the Christ talked about the Kingdom of God, the common people understood that he was not referring to the kingdom of Caesar or the kingdom of Babylon, that He was talking about a kingdom that was very different from a worldly kingdom. The Kingdom of God is not a church, a religion, or a political organization. It has *nothing* to do with any worldly *ism* whatsoever. The Kingdom of God is the Kingdom of the Light, a field of sheer brilliant Light that has always existed and will always exist, and because of certain cosmic reasons it is now coming closer to Earth.

This is why the whole of Humanity is presently at a crossroad, a testing and trial period. First of all, individuals are being tested as to whether or not they are fit to enter the Kingdom of God individually, and different groups around the planet, both religious and esoteric, are being tested if they can enter as a group. They are being tested by the measure of Light—how much Light they have individually and as a group. No one can cheat the Light; the Light "knows" whether you are ready or not. You cannot say, "I've been a faithful follower for so many years, therefore I must deserve the Light." You cannot deserve the Light unless you *are* the Light. It is not a mental concept; it is a transformation inside you, what you *are* inside.

In this day and age, unfortunately, everything goes through the mind. Those who are educated in psychology, philosophy, science and other fields try to find solutions to all problems through their mind. It is all a field of mental activity that is perfectly natural for the way human beings have evolved until now, but it does not qualify them to enter the Kingdom of the Light, no matter how clever they are, because the Light is of a different quality from the mind. The mind is just part of one's personality: it is still materialistic, still the vibration of Matter. The Light is a much higher vibration, a subtle, fine *energy*, and the only way you can connect your personality with the Light is through the Light itself. There is no other way. Mind cannot do it, emotions cannot do it, physical vitality cannot do it—nothing can do it but Light itself.

The important thing is that you must gather Light. When people go to a spiritual retreat they receive Light and they absorb the Light, which gives them a chance to actually move ahead on the Path. But then they go home and they get swamped by their worldly concerns (their family, job, environment and all kinds of problems), and slowly that Light they received diminishes until it disappears and they are back to their normal worldly vibration. This means that they did not connect strongly enough to the Light to maintain it. If the Light is blazing inside you all the time no matter what goes on, then you know that you have connected to the Light.

At a certain point the Light becomes irreversible: it shines inside you all the time, twenty-four hours a day, undisturbed by what you do or do not do. Whether you are sick or healthy, happy or not happy makes no difference; circumstances will not change the Light inside you.

People in an esoteric school are lucky because they are given a much greater chance than the average person in the world. In the world there are only the churches and the orthodox religions, which can give you a certain amount of Light and can point the way towards Reality. But in an esoteric school you are given much more than an orthodox view of life: you are given Esoteric Knowledge, which gives you an understanding of why you are really here, what you should be doing and what your vision or goal should be. So people who belong to an esoteric school have a tremendous advantage over the others, but even they cannot qualify until they have the Light strong, bright and clear inside them.

It is important to make an all-out effort to connect to the Light and remain in the Light because the days are coming when you won't be able to do it. Christ said, "Walk in the Light while you have the Light because the days are coming when you will not have the Light anymore" *(John* 12: 35). In other words, you have to have the Light before the bad days arrive, because during those times, circumstances will be such that you will not be able to access it.

Gāyatrī: The Destroyer of Darkness

The Gāyatrī Mantra is essentially the Destroyer of Darkness. To understand this we have to understand what Darkness is. Darkness is everything that is not Light, everything that is not of the pure vibration of Absolute Reality referred to by Saint John: "God is Light and in Him there is no darkness at all" *(John* 1: 5). This is only half the truth because God is also Darkness. What Saint John was trying to say was the same as what the Gāyatrī Mantra tells us: move towards the Light; that is where the Path leads. Once you reach your goal, you will understand that God is also Darkness.

Everything that is not Light is Darkness. This means that your physical body and the Physical World, your emotional body and the Astral World, and your mental body and the Mental World are Darkness. They are Darkness because they are not of the frequency of Light. Now, the Gāyatrī is the Destroyer of Darkness; it is the *power* of Light itself. Everything that is negative, in Nature and in you, is of the Darkness, which is the other half of the Deity. If you don't like it and don't want to work with it, you can call upon the other part of the Deity, which is Light. Light destroys Darkness.

There is a practical application in this. The Gāyatrī destroys Darkness, so if you are in a bad mood, which is darkness, how are you going to destroy it? With the Gāyatrī. If you are not physically well, how are you going to destroy it? With the Gāyatrī. In other words, if you want to improve your health or overcome negative emotions or thoughts, use the Gāyatrī Mantra; it will overcome everything which is of the Darkness. It can be a powerful tool in your life, if you use it. It will not only transform your life on the personality level but also give you a ladder that leads you to the Source, the Soul Realm within you.

So, whenever you are in a negative condition or situation, or when a tragedy happens in your life, just repeat and meditate on the Gāyatrī Mantra.[10] Immediately you will begin to feel that fine filament of Light working. It does not mean that the tragedy will disappear; if somebody close to you has died it does not mean that they're going to be resurrected for you. No, but what happens is that your internal consciousness undergoes a modification and understands from the point of view of Light, not from the point of view of Darkness. Everything you experience in your normal state is from the point of view of Darkness. When the Gāyatrī energy is functioning inside you, everything you experience is from the point of view of Light. You can see what is good or bad, real or false, important or not important, temporary or eternal. In other words, you have an inner way of knowing that annihilates every kind of ignorance. But it doesn't mean that the Darkness won't exist. It will exist; it has to. But the important thing is that your relationship to the Darkness will change.

Then, you will understand that Darkness always opposes Light, and that is the way it should be; it is all part of the Divine Plan. In other words, nothing will ever bother you anymore because you will understand that the Light, the Darkness and the misery down here are exactly the same thing. Everything is the One Reality; whatever is happening is the one unimaginable, vast Reality working in different ways, in different realms, for different purposes—but ultimately it is the same One Reality.

10. Because of its sacred nature, the Gāyatrī Mantra must be received by direct transmission from a Teacher. For a word-by-word explanation of the mantra, see: Imre Vallyon, *The New Planetary Reality* (Sounding-Light Publishing, 2012), 83–88; but an audio file giving the intonation of the mantra is not provided in that book or this one. If you feel moved to receive the mantra through the proper channels, you can start the process by going to the website of our Spiritual School (www.planetarytransformation.org). However, a good alternative is to practise the *Invocation to the Forces of Light* that follows this chapter. This is an invocation to the very same Light-Energy of the Gāyatrī Mantra. (Ed.)

This is the *Way of Understanding that Leads to Peace.* This understanding is not a mental knowing but something beyond anything that you can imagine. When you are on that level of Understanding, you have a field of knowledge that, whatever happens, past, present, or future, it always leads you to Peace; a superior knowledge that transforms everything that happens to you into Peace.

This *Peace* is not the peace of the world. Christ said, "I give you my peace, not the peace of the world" *(John* 14: 27). This *Peace* means total Peace: the Peace of the Absolute, the Peace that is the origin of the whole Cosmic Manifestation. Capital-p Peace does not refer to when you stop fighting with somebody. That is not Peace. Capital-p Peace means the peace of the Buddha and the Christ, the peace of Kṛṣna, Moses, Mohammed, Lao Tzu and everybody who has ever *attained.* It is an internal structure of indestructible steadiness. Everything can fall apart around and inside you—your body, mind and the world can fall apart—but this Peace remains solid and immovable. That is the *Peace* we mean here.

PRACTICE

Invocation to the Forces of Light

Ōṁ Gāyatraī Devyaī Namaha

Gāyatrī represents all the Forces of Light that emanate from the Sun. If you look at a close-up of our Sun, you will see a pulsating, living sphere of beautiful orange, red and yellow. It's alive and continually moving, a massive, seething ball of fire. That ball of fire gives us light in the world on the physical dimension level. We can live because of that beautiful radiation of fire from the Sun—even on the physical level.

So the Sun has a physical body, which you can see and feel, but like us it has internal bodies: an astral part, a mental part, a causal part and so on. In the higher realms, the Sun is a dynamic, boundless Light-Field from which all the Light energies pour into all the visible and invisible planets in the Solar System. The invisible planets are in the Astral, Mental, Causal, Buddhic and Nirvāṇic Worlds, part of the massive Solar-Systemic structure. The planets are really Chakras, or energy-fields, within the body of the Sun and are fed and nourished by the Boundless Light-Field, which is Gāyatrī.

Glory be to you, Solar Logos;
Glory be to you, Spiritual Sun.
In you we live, move and have our being,
In the Light of our Lord, the Sun.

This is an invocation to the Divine Light-Field, which starts off at the innermost part of the Sun and goes through the various planes and finally manifests on the physical level as the wonderful, pulsating, yellow-orange ball of fire we call the Sun. All the Forces of Light emanate from the Sun and with this intonation we are concerned with invoking those Forces, which will help us through our whole lives, making us healthy and happy, helping us get in tune with our destiny.

When we talk about invoking the *Forces* of Light we are talking about real Forces, entities and hierarchies that work with Light: Angelic Hierarchies, Archangelic Hierarchies and the Hierarchies of the DEVAS, the "Shining Ones", who can manipulate the forces of Light. These hierarchies are consciously aware that they are living in the body of the Solar Logos, and when we can also be aware that we are part of the Solar Logos, we will have achieved human perfection and become what we are supposed to be: conscious creators with the Deity working on the Divine Plan for the evolution of Humanity and the planet.

In the invocation, GĀYATRAĪ means "to the Forces of Light" and DEVYAĪ means "divine", from DEVA, the "Shining Ones or the "Divine Ones". Both words are in their feminine form, however, so the Light being invoked is the Feminine Light, the soft Light of the Buddhic dimension, what the Christian Mystics called SERENA LUX, the Serene Light—as against the bright Father Light. You cannot enter into the all-powerful brilliance of that Light unless the soft Feminine Light is strong inside you.

While you intone the following Mantra, think of Light, which is like a scintillating feeling inside you, in your energy-field, your aura, and try to fill yourself with the Divine Feminine Light.[11]

ŌṀ GĀYATRAĪ DEVYAĪ NAMAHA

11. An audio file demonstrating the correct intonation of this mantra can be found at www.planetary-transformation.org/mantrarepetition.

Spiritual Warfare

At the moment, the planet is at a crisis point—well, the planet has always been at a crisis point; it's just a matter of what degree of crisis. This is the planet of crises, but sometimes there are bigger crises than normal. The First World War, for instance, was a big crisis, the Second World War was a big crisis, and this is an even bigger crisis.

In the Lemurian Age, millions of years ago, the crisis point had to do with the development of the physical body, how Humanity reacted to the outside world, the physical dimension, because in the early days of Lemuria people did not react to the physical world properly. In Atlantean days, the crisis point was about our emotional development, whether we could sense right and wrong, good and evil, happiness and misery. In other words, whether we had evolved enough according to the Divine Plan, a part of which was the perfection of the astral body, the sensitive mechanism whereby humans could feel things. The crisis point now has to do with the mental development of the ĀRYAN race.[12]

By the way, you probably think the word ĀRYAN has something to do with Hitler, but it is a Sanskrit word meaning "noble one", "one who has attained self-mastery", "one who has reached oneness with himself and the environment". It has nothing to do with Hitler. Similarly, the SVASTIKA was used in the East to denote the manifestation of the Divine Presence, and the Buddhists in all the Asiatic countries still use

12. For details regarding the human evolutionary epochs and the actual meaning of the Āryan race, see Imre Vallyon, *Heavens and Hells of the Mind*, i. 176–179.

it. But Hitler decided to use the word Āryan and the Svastika symbol for his Nazi Party. They adapted words and symbols for their own use—like the Christians adapted the cross, the Jews adapted the six-pointed star, the Muslims adapted the crescent and the star—without even understanding what they really mean.

Coming back to the crisis of this particular age, the Āryan Age, the crisis point is about the mind, and this is where the warfare is. At the moment, the evolution of Humanity has reached a crisis point because the mind is overshadowing the Soul.

Originally, the mind, or the mental body, was devised so that humans could think, plan, reason, assess things and work things out. That's what the mind is supposed to do, and there's nothing wrong with that. But the problem now is that the mind is overused to such a point that it completely shuts out the Light of the Soul. The activity of the mental body of the average person today completely neutralizes any Light the Soul tries to send through to that person on the personality level. So, the crisis point today is about the mental development of humans.

I call this *Spiritual Warfare.*

Christians have the expression "spiritual warfare", but to them it means they are fighting against everybody who is not of their particular group or sect, whether they are evangelicals, Pentecostals, fundamentalists or whatever. The Muslims are also waging "spiritual warfare", which they call *jihad.* And what do they do? They blow people up, including themselves, and that to them is spiritual warfare.

Notice that these two groups, the Christians and the Muslims, have completely warped the idea of Spiritual Warfare.

Spiritual Warfare, on the level of the individual, is the battle between the Soul and the personality. The Soul is trying to get control of the personality because the personality is in control and it negates the Soul. On a worldwide scale, the whole planet is under pressure from the Soul of the World, the Anima Mundi, which is trying to make an impression on the human species but cannot get through the massive, mental energy-field of Humanity. Because billions of people are "educated"—they have developed their minds and continually use them—they throw off a huge amount of mental energy into the planetary atmosphere. That in itself becomes a problem because the Light of the Buddhic World, the Light of Higher Perception, cannot penetrate through to the personality level. So we have what *we* call Spiritual Warfare, warfare between the Soul and the personality.

Now, this is happening inside you, in all religious groups, in all spiritual schools, everywhere around the planet, because it is part of the Divine Plan. The Divine Plan at the moment is for the Soul to control the personality.

During the last six thousand years, Spiritual Warfare was fought individually. The Buddha did it, Rāma did it, Kṛṣna did it and all the great Saints and Avatāras did it. They went out into the desert, the mountains and caves and meditated and fought a huge internal battle until the Soul won. Buddha sat under a tree until his Soul totally mastered his personality. It was an individual battle. That was in the past, but now the battle is on a planetary scale. The whole planet is struggling now because that is what the New Age is about. What we did in the past as individuals in different parts of the planet, we now do in groups and we do it on a planetary scale.

We are trying to tell you that this is a crisis point for the planet and for everybody who is participating in it, and how things turn out for the planet will be decided within the next two or three hundred years. If within that time millions of people en masse have not switched over to Soul control, then Humanity will be going back into a dark age, worse than ever because the mind principle will totally annihilate any sense of feeling. Remember, *the mind does not feel.* People who commit vicious crimes have no feeling; they work only through the mind. Dictators around the world work through their minds; they have an idea and they do it no matter what the cost. Scientists can perform cruel research on animals because they work though the mind. If the mental development goes so far that people lose any sense of heart or feeling, this civilization is going to descend into the most negative civilization in the history of Mankind.

The same thing is happening in esoteric groups, including ours, and it is also happening in religious groups that are dominated by the mind, instead of the Soul: the mind is annihilating sensitivity toward the Soul. Such groups will have to undergo a process of Purification, meaning that individually and on the group level the Soul battles to overcome mental impressions, manifesting as a battle between those who think that spiritual life is just a mental idea and those who actually see and experience the Light of the Soul and surrender to that Light within themselves.

If you are in a spiritual school or on the Spiritual Path, you have to go through Spiritual Warfare to sort out whether you are fit for the New Revelation or not. Some battles are bigger and some smaller but everybody without exception has to go through them. It doesn't matter how long you have belonged to a school or how long you have studied. You may not have studied anything but if you have a good relationship with your Soul, you will get there. If you have studied everything under the sun and have no relationship with your Soul, you won't get there. This is hard for intellectuals to understand because they think that the more ideas they have, the more enlightened they are. They are not. Ideas can be useful, yes, definitely. They can be put into practice and used for something. But ideas themselves, no matter how clever, do not connect *you* to your *Soul.* We are talking about something else—Spiritual Warfare, the battle between what you-the-Soul wants and what you-the-personality wants.

You have to understand that you are in a state of warfare and that produces stress inside you. When your personality is fighting your Soul, you are under stress. When the total human family, seven billion people, are fighting against the World Soul, then Humanity is under stress. This is why we have endless wars and social problems. It is all part of the war between the personality of Humanity and the Soul of Humanity, the great World Soul that we are all part of, what in Sanskrit is called PARAMĀTMAN, the Supreme Self, the One Self or the All-Self.

The World Soul is trying to overwhelm the myriads of little personalities, and the Soul inside you is struggling to overwhelm your personality impulses. This will create some stress in your life, concerning your job, family, the situation you're living in—what we call natural stress from your environment. And you will remain stressed out until you resolve the conflict and understand that this stress is a good thing for you because it indicates the direction you should be going. You will never be happy unless you connect to your Soul. Once you understand that, it is no longer a stress but a challenge. You say, "Okay, I'm feeling this way because I'm out of tune with my Soul. So what do I do to get in tune with my Soul?"

This is where the importance of practice comes in, because spiritual life is not just an idea in your head; you have to *live* it. There are many groups, even esoteric groups, that have good ideas and esoteric knowledge but they have no spiritual practices to go with their knowledge. You have to have something practical, like dynamic mantric energies, meditation practices, breathing techniques, and so on. With practice you open yourself up to the Light and enable the Soul to bring down the Light because you are communicating with it. When you practice a mantra, for example, in effect you are talking to your Soul, and the Soul understands perfectly what you are trying to say because *your Soul knows the mantra*. Every mantra comes from the level of the Soul, so the Soul responds to the mantric energy. Then you receive the Soul Light and it becomes a part of your *way*, your possibility for personal transformation.

Spiritual techniques like those in this book will give you a means and process for how to reconnect to your Soul. But do you know what the joke is? You actually *are* the Soul; you are that. The funny thing is that you think that the Soul is something "up there", separate from you, and you have to get *there*. What you have forgotten is that you already are the Soul; in fact, *this*—the personality—is the one that is not the real self. Your personality is the unreal part of you, that which just comes and goes and changes like the weather. The real part of you is that which you are struggling to get to; that's the joke. It's all part of the *Great Delusion*.

What is Enlightenment?

First of all, Enlightenment has to do with knowledge. On the personality level, if you are living an ordinary life with lots of problems and somebody comes along and tells you something which gels inside you so that you change your way of life—that is a form of Enlightenment. When you go from kindergarten to grade school you are enlightened because you move from a lower knowledge level to a higher knowledge level. When you move from school to university you are enlightened because you have more knowledge than you previously had.

Let's consider the so-called Age of Enlightenment. Following the first 250 years after the death of Christ, every form of knowledge was suppressed by the Church. The Church authorities suppressed the Gnostics, the Alchemists, the Masons, the Rosicrucians, the Kabbalists, the Illuminati and other groups who did not want to believe only what the Church told them. That suppression went on for many centuries, right through the Middle Ages, the so-called Dark Ages, and then in the seventeenth and eighteenth centuries came the Age of Enlightenment. People started to think for themselves and created new forms of music, art and science, new ways of looking at the world, new ideas of how society should work, how people should be free from the Church and think for themselves. In other words, the Mind Principle started functioning in Humanity on a large scale and hundreds of millions of people were in the process of enlightenment, or expanding their knowledge.

Now, you have probably heard about the Enlightenment of the Buddha. According to the Buddhists, Buddha went into the condition of Nirvāṇa and that was Enlightenment. So many people in the world, including Westerners, think that Enlightenment is entry into Nirvāṇa.[13] Another view of Enlightenment is that of the Hindu yogis. They call it Self-Realization, when you realize your Self, the Soul that you are, and disjoin yourself from the personality condition. And then there is the Enlightenment of Ramana Mahārṣi, who entered into the Kingdom of the Heart at the age of fourteen and stayed in that condition until the end of his life.

Notice that with these examples of entering Nirvāṇa, Self-Realization or the Heart Condition, there is no change after that. Buddha went into Nirvāṇa and did not go anywhere else. Ramana Mahārṣi went into the Heart and stayed there. The yogis attained Self-Realization and remained on that level. All these examples indicate that Enlightenment is some kind of *fixed* attainment. It is the same with the Christian Mystics of the first two and a half centuries of Christianity, who also attained the Heart Condition. They united themselves with the Christ in the Heart, but they also stayed there until they died. Again it was a fixed condition.

This is also the history of all the religions, whether it is Buddhism, Christianity, Hinduism, or the religions of China and Persia. For them, Enlightenment is the knowledge-field they were given at a particular time. For the Persians, what Zoroaster taught was Enlightenment; for the Christians, what the Christ taught was Enlightenment; for the

13. Nirvāṇa is a particular condition but not what the Buddhists think it is. They think Nirvāṇa is an annihilation, a destruction of everything into some sort of a condition where there is no suffering or sorrow. But that is a negative view of Nirvāṇa. The real Nirvāṇa is a world of Light, an incredibly *positive* experience. In any case, even if you understand Nirvāṇa correctly, it is just one idea of Enlightenment.

Buddhists, what the Buddha taught was Enlightenment; and for the Chinese, what Confucius taught was Enlightenment—at that time. But they all became stuck.

The Pope, the Dalai Lama and other religious leaders follow a tradition that is repeated unaltered. The Jewish tradition is 5,000 years old, the Christian tradition is more than 2,000 years old, the Buddhist tradition is 2,500 years old and the Muslim tradition is about 1,500 years old. A tradition becomes fixed somewhere along the line and for centuries after, people in authority repeat that same fixation. They do the same old rituals and tell the same old stories over and over again, stories that should have been discarded thousands of years ago. Stuck!

It is the same in any esoteric group. Whether it's the Theosophical Society, the Masonic tradition, the Rosicrucians, Kabbalists or Alchemists, they reach a certain point of knowledge—they are enlightened to a certain point—but then they become fixed. In Indian ashrams they may have one mantra or one breathing technique, and they keep working with that over and over again. They do not know that other systems exist even within their own tradition or religion, let alone all the other knowledge that exists in the world. It's hard to explain how stuck human beings really are!

This applies to science also. Science is part of the expanding field of knowledge (or Enlightenment) because it explains how things work on the physical level—how atoms work, how steam works, how electricity works—and that is good. But science got stuck in the nineteenth century when they declared there was no God, no Soul or Spirit, no invisible worlds or energies. Everything that could not be proven by a mathematical formula was nonsense. And science is still stuck because scientists still refuse to believe that there may be something beyond the physical, material structure that they are continually tearing apart and examining.

The point is that most people, whatever their understanding of Enlightenment, think it is something final, something fixed.

The real Esoteric Masters say that there is no such thing as a fixed Enlightenment; every point of knowledge is good, every point of knowledge is right and beneficial, and there is no point of knowledge where you remain fixed forever and ever. It simply means that Knowledge is eternal and infinite, that the Mind of God is eternal and infinite. And Enlightenment means that you bring down that section of the Knowledge that you require at that time, for that age, for yourself, for society, for the evolutionary process of Humanity. Enlightenment is not once and for all a final thing; it is an ever-moving process, like a river, the River of Consciousness that moves ever onward.

Here is my understanding of Enlightenment:

Wherever your consciousness is focused, there is your Enlightenment.

This means that if you're concentrating on Nirvāṇa, that is your Enlightenment; if you're concentrating on your Higher Self, or Soul, that is your Enlightenment; if you're concentrating on understanding how electricity works, that is your Enlightenment. Enlightenment is always a process of *understanding*. The big secret is that there is no limit or end to it—no finality.

If there were something such as a final field of knowledge or Enlightenment beyond which you cannot go, what would you do for the next four billion years of evolution? Can you imagine the absolute boredom? Can you imagine the Buddha sitting in Nirvāṇa for four billion years? Or the Christ sitting next to His Father on a throne listening to the angels playing harps? Harp music is very nice but listening to it for four billion years would drive you nuts. Enlightenment has no beginning and no end. You can put your attention on something and absorb whatever knowledge you can from it, and then move on to the next thing.

The Mind of God is not something fixed! If the Mind of God were fixed it would be an absolute disaster for the Cosmos: there would be no evolution; there would be no progress; there would be nothing. But the Mind of God is open and infinite. This is difficult for people to understand because they like to be fixed on something. Humans like to go along the ways they know. Science, religion, philosophy, all human thinking gets stuck. The very charm of old universities like Oxford or Cambridge is precisely that they are set in their ways.

To be stuck on something is not the right idea because it means that you are putting yourself out of the moving stream. The Knowledge-Field is always moving; it is not a rock that was wedged in place two, three or six thousand years ago. If you cannot change you become a rock obstructing the flow; you can no longer move with the Knowledge-Field, the field of Experience. But if you understand what real Enlightenment is, you will understand that whatever stage you have reached you can move on, whatever stage anyone has reached they can move on and whatever stage human evolution has reached it can move on.

Our School is based on the immediate present. My mission is to teach the Knowledge-Field in the immediate moment, not to repeat an old tradition. When we started the School we could have chosen a particular way, like the Kabbalah, the Divine Names, the Gāyatrī or another Eastern teaching, and repeated exactly the same thing over and over again. We could have been happy and we could call ourselves enlightened. But I would have died in the process. I could not possibly do that. Since I was born until now, my mind has been completely open; it has no limitations or structured forms of learning. Therefore I can have fresh knowledge and fresh awareness about everything, on the spot.

Great Teachers like Lao Tzu and Krishnamurti had minds that were not cluttered, that were completely open to receive new ways of understanding the old subjects. The subjects are always the same—God, the Universe, human beings have always been here. But what you can teach is what the truly enlightened have: a new way of *seeing*. With minds that are uncluttered and open like an ocean, they are able to bring in new information and a new understanding of the subject, whatever it is.

That is why there are very few Esoteric Teachers in the world. If you look at any tradition, there is always a particular system and a particular method is handed down from one teacher to the next. There are very few Schools in the world that are limitless and open to the infinitude of Knowing. Try to find a Teacher like me who is always open and not simply passing on a tradition. Esoteric schools and esoteric teachers are extraordinarily rare on this planet *and always have been.*

Before starting our School, I used to teach occult groups and when I brought up the idea that I would like to unite the Esoteric Wisdom of the West and the Esoteric Wisdom of the East into one knowledge-field, they told me it could not be done. When you are following an old tradition, the idea of uniting the East and the West into one field of knowledge seems impossible, but I thought it was possible because at that time my mind was already embracing the All-Knowledge Field.

We *did* unite the East and the West and we can work with both energy-streams as long as we allow the School to be in the eternal Knowledge-Field of the moment, which is a kind of Light-Energy, the pulsation of the Understanding of the Deity Itself. We're moving with the immediate Understanding, not something that was said and done in the past. We are always open to the Light, the movement of Light-Intelligence in the Cosmos, as it is in the moment. In this way we can move forward as a living stream of energy in the Mind of God and bring the evolution of Humanity ever forward toward the Light.

The Reason for Getting Stuck

I mentioned previously that all religions get stuck, all esoteric groups and spiritual schools get stuck, sciences, philosophies and social systems get stuck. No matter how wonderful the religion or science, no matter how wonderful the philosophy or knowledge, people get stuck and we have to understand why. It is not the fault of any one system or any one group or society. It is not anyone's fault; it is a *fact*, an existential fact of life.

When people first thought up the idea of Communism it was good. Communal living, sharing things, everybody is equal, no aristocracy, no bourgeoisie—they were all bright ideas that were going to change the world. Until they put them into practice and created absolute dictatorships. The pattern is often the same: a system starts with a fresh idea that is originally good, that comes from inspired people, but then the human beings get stuck and that is the end of it. Democracy was originally good but nowadays it too is stuck.

Essentially, you have to look at this phenomenon of being stuck because you may also have the same situation in your life. You can get stuck in your relationship and in your attitude at work. Being stuck is universal. So what is the phenomenon of being stuck, and why does it arise in the first place?

The Conflict is between the Past and the Future, and between Spirit and Matter.

The conflict is always between the past and the future. What connects the past and the future is the Eternal Moment, the Living Moment in the here and now, which is a totally timeless condition. In *this* moment, in this very second, there is no past and no future, just what *is*. And if you can live in this very second, then you can understand the Light-Energy that is flowing now, the *enlightening* energy that is right here, right now. If you cannot live in the here and now, you are in the past. (The future hasn't arisen yet, so you can't be in the future.) Because people cannot be in the Living Moment, they are always referring back to the past, what they already know, what they did, how they were before—because that is what they can understand and relate to. So they are in the past; they are stuck.

This is a basic conflict of human existence. I'm talking about the human consciousness only; the animals do not have this problem because they are not conscious of the past, present and future. The angels do not have it either, because the *real* angels (not the "angel guides" of the channellers) sense time as a continuum, not what happened in the past or what will happen in the future, just one event flowing into the next. Only the human species, the human consciousness, has this problem of being stuck in the past.

And as I said, this is widespread amongst all religions, all groups, all societies, all political parties. Humanity itself is stuck. But there is nobody to blame; it is just about understanding why something is the way it is and then trying to remedy it according to what you can do. It is easy to blame others; that does not require any qualifications. But to understand the situation does require qualifications, a true understanding that this phenomenon of being stuck has to do with not being able to be in the moment, in other words, not being able to flow with the current of Life.

If you can live moment by moment you will always be in the eternal continuum of Knowing: understanding the energies and forces working inside and outside of you *now*; understanding what those energies and forces are doing to your environment *now*; what they are doing to your country *now*; what they are doing to the world *now*. As your understanding grows your perception becomes vaster, and *that* is the way of the Spirit. If you are connected to that internally, you are always at peace.

This is one part of the conflict. The other part, which is bigger and more esoteric, is the conflict between Spirit and Matter.[14]

So there is the problem of Time, which is eternal and is split into the past, the milliseconds of the present, and the future. And then there is the problem of Space, in which Spirit and Matter exist in the same space. And here another big conflict arises: the conflict between Matter, which always holds on to the past, and Spirit, which is always in the future.

Matter wants to stay where it is, to do exactly the same thing all the time. The very fact that something exists in Matter shows that it is of the past, crystallized, stuck. But Matter *has* to be stuck, otherwise Creation could not be held together. Imagine if the matter of planet Earth decided to change and move all over the place all the time. There would be chaos and the whole planet would disintegrate. Your physical body has to be stuck, otherwise its atoms would not be held together and you would disintegrate physically. So the very nature of Matter is to be organized and stay together, and be stuck.

14. As mentioned previously, everything is Spirit. But here we differentiate between Spirit and Matter. *Matter* (capitalized) refers to the whole substance of the Physical World, Astral World and Mental World, which are the lowest vibrations of Spirit. When we use the term *the Spirit*, we refer to a particular level of Spirit: Nirvāṇa, which is the home of Ātman, the Spirit.

But Spirit is not like that. Spirit is the opposite: it is boundless and free, eternally in the future, an ever-flowing movement of Reality.

Now, Humanity is in the middle of the conflict between Spirit and Matter. This is symbolized by the Cross, which represents Humanity crucified between Spirit and Matter. As a human being, therefore, you are on a cross between Spirit and Matter, and how much you are bound to Matter determines your state of bondage, and how much you are with Spirit determines your state of Liberation. If your consciousness is limited to your physical body, you are very much in the past. If your consciousness is limited to your thinking process, you are a bit more advanced. But if your consciousness is not limited by your body or your mind, if it is not limited even by your Soul, you are an enlightened Buddha or Christ, or an Adept, a Master or a Saint—what everybody will be when they have discarded their material bondage or limitations. The closer you are to the Spirit, the more enlightened you are, the more in the future you are.

People who are stuck in the past are so stuck in matter that they cannot change anything; they do not want to change anything. They are quite happy doing exactly what they have been doing. We call that cultural conditioning. But even that is changing nowadays. Even Matter is being shaken up and the closed structure of being stuck is no longer quite possible because the Spirit is pushing down from its home in Nirvāṇa, stirring up Matter so that it cannot have the same degree of crystallization as in the past, even though it always wants to be the same.

So everybody will have to change. You have to change, science has to change, society has to change, the planet has to change.

The process of crystallization caused by the structure of Matter itself is no longer able to function as it did for hundreds of thousands of years. That process is no longer valid. The Spirit, which is like an ever-flowing, eternal Knowing-Action field, does not want to be limited by Matter; it wants to move everything forward. And because of that there will be many natural disasters—earthquakes, volcanoes, hurricanes, tornados, floods—as part of the shake-up of physical matter. But there is also a shake-up on the Soul level, the mental level and the emotional level. All the structures of the Inner Worlds are being shaken by the force of the Spirit, the Boundless Ocean of Spiritual Energy, as it slowly filters down through the inner dimensions to the physical level.

And it will express itself in many ways in the Physical World. People are already being shaken in countries all over the world. There are all kinds of political movements and rebellions, people marching in European countries and Arab countries wanting change. They want more money, more jobs, but they do not understand that there is actually a spirit of change moving across the whole planet. And it has nothing to do with money or jobs. People will have to change their way of thinking and doing things, whether they like it or not. If they don't like it there are going to be many problems, and much conflict. Conflict will arise between the old forces of crystallization that do not want to change and the new forces that understand the change, whether consciously or subconsciously, and want to move along with it.

I mentioned previously that there could be a huge conflict with the Muslim world, which is a giant rock stopping the movement of Life because it is far behind the energy stream of the Moment. But it's not only the Muslims; there are also ultra-orthodox Jewish sects, fundamentalist Christians and other groups that are still way behind in the stream of Evolution. The stream is all-powerful; it will destroy the rocks, no matter how hard they are. It keeps flowing over them, slowly wearing them down until the rocks are turned to pebbles. So the great, mighty Energy coming from the Spirit will pulverize every opposition in time. It is irresistible. The force of Spirit wins over Matter, no matter how much Matter resists it. So the wisest thing is to just go along with it.

And as I said the Spirit has a vision of the future. The Spirit *is* the future. The Spirit knows what something *should be*, not just what it is. It is like an architect who designs a house and knows where the bathrooms, bedrooms and furnishings are going to be. *The Spirit has the Plan.* It knows the finished product, how the Universe will be, and it has the *authority* to make sure that it is going to be like that, just like the architect makes sure that the workers have put everything in the right place. So sooner or later everybody and everything will have to fit in with that Plan. The Spirit, in esoteric language, is the Master Builder, the Great Architect of the Universe.

The Human Hierarchy is the link between Spirit and Matter. We are the only hierarchy in Creation that unites the lowest level of Matter with the highest level of Spirit, so if we cannot invoke the Spirit, who can? It is our job to bring the Light-Energy of the Spirit down to help all of Mankind; to spread that Light and Energy, that Understanding and Wisdom, so that it shines in the planetary atmosphere and impacts millions of people, whether they know it or not. We spread the Light and the Light will do the Work as it needs to be done for that particular time and location, for those particular people and situations.

PRACTICE

Visualizing the Rose in the Heart

This meditation is called *Visualizing the Rose in the Heart.* This is an important meditation that will help you develop the right qualification for doing spiritual work.

Before you can do spiritual work your solar plexus has to be calm. This is why this visualization starts at the Solar Plexus Centre. With your attention focused in the Solar Plexus Centre, you visualize a green stem and green branches and leaves. They are all the beautiful, young, fresh green of spring. Then, visualize a soft-pink-coloured rose at the top of the stem, in the Heart Centre. Do not try imagining other colours you prefer; you have to give up your personal ideas. The stem is green and starts at the Solar Plexus Centre, with green branches and leaves moving up to the Heart Centre, where there is a big, soft pink rose.

The reason that the stem of the rose starts in your Solar Plexus Centre is that the solar plexus is where all your troubles lie, in terms of personal relationships. By visualizing the green leaves and branches starting there, you're telling your solar plexus that you want it to be quiet and peaceful, since green is the colour that gives the solar plexus tranquillity and peace. The pink colour of the rose awakens the Love aspect of your Heart. So this visualization does two things for you: it pacifies your solar plexus and awakens the Love of the Heart; in other words, it tells your solar plexus that whatever emotional moods you have are to move up to the Heart and be transmuted in the Love of the Heart.

These two work together: if your solar plexus is active, the Love of the Heart is inactive; if the Love of the Heart is active, the solar plexus is calm. A person's solar plexus is normally active, so most people are not connected to the Heart. This visualization will establish a permanent connection between your solar plexus and the Heart, and after a while the Heart will dominate the whole process, which is the ultimate aim of this exercise. Then your Heart Chakra will be open and your solar plexus will be calm all the time.

So assume a comfortable sitting position in a quiet environment and have nothing in your mind except that you are going to visualize this rose, with its stem and leaves. Do not analyse it, criticize it or think about its meaning. Just see the vision of the *Rose in the Heart* and hold it. And do it in your own time.

PART III

The Way of the Mystery School

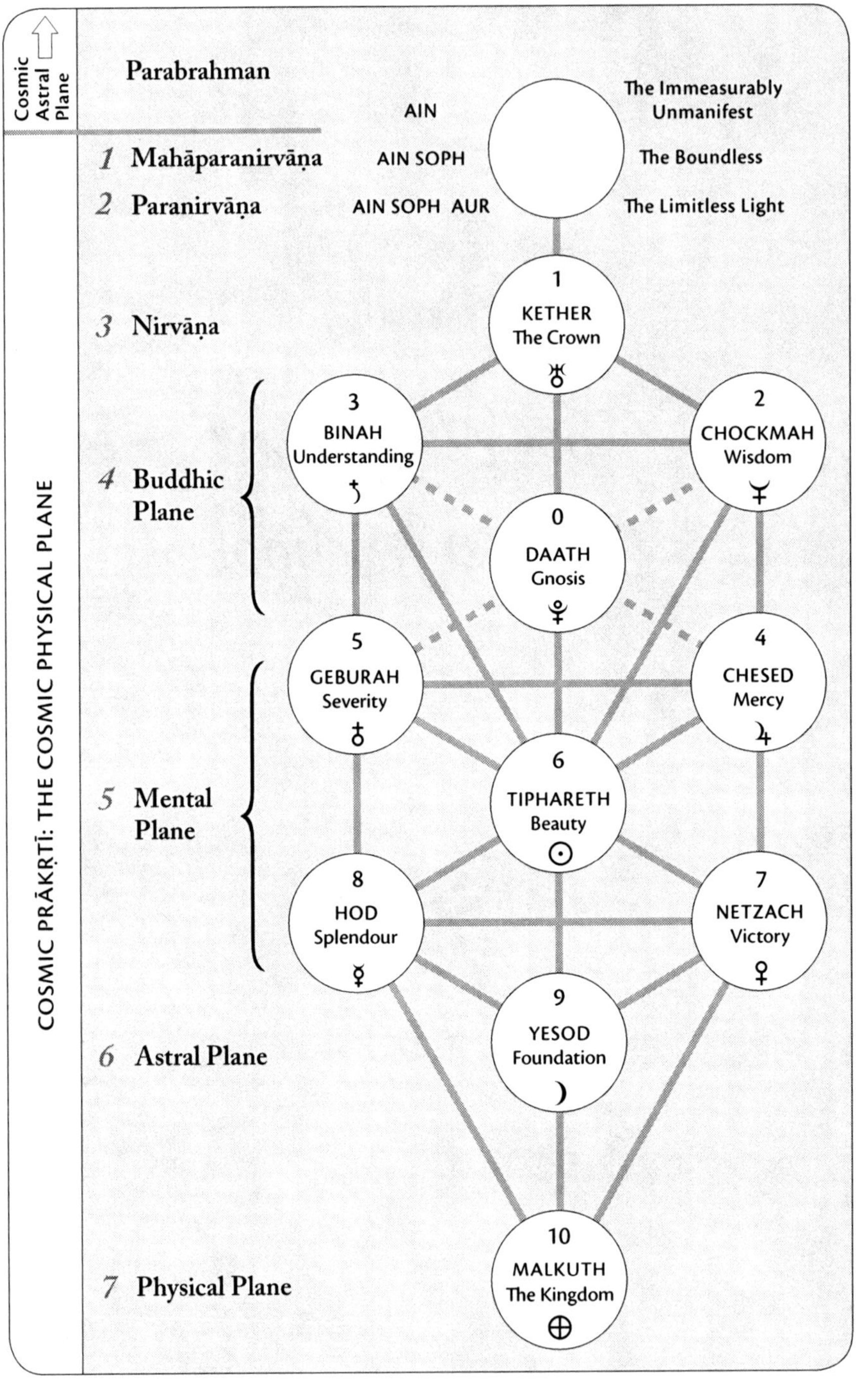

The Planes and the Kabbalistic Tree of Life

A Brief Explanation of the Tree of Life

Knowledge of the Tree of Life is a fundamental part of the Mystery School system, so we will start with a brief explanation of what the Tree of Life is and how it works.

The Tree of Life[15] is a map of you and the Universe you live in—the outer worlds and the Inner Worlds. If you are in an unfamiliar city and do not have a map, it will be difficult to know where you are or to find the place you are trying to get to. So people who do not have a map of the inner dimensions face the same situation: they have inner experiences during meditation without knowing what they are experiencing or how to relate one experience to another. In India, for example, they do not know about the Tree of Life because it is not a part of their tradition. So they have no map, which means they do not know where they are when they have inner experiences. They might experience themselves as the Soul, for example, and think that they are great Avatāras or incarnations of God, when in reality they are only halfway up the Tree of Life.

The base of the Tree of Life is MALKUTH (the Kingdom), which represents your physical body and the physical world around you. The next level is YESOD (the Foundation), which is the Astral World. But between the Kingdom and the Foundation there are what we call the etheric-physical subplanes (which are technically part of the Physical

15. Refer to the adjacent diagram *The Planes and the Kabbalistic Tree of Life*. Keep in mind that this is only a two-dimensional representation of a multidimensional reality that cannot be depicted in a flat figure.

World and are therefore not shown in the diagram of the Tree of Life). Because they are invisible, you cannot sense them with your physical body but you can with your etheric-physical body. When you meditate you may have nonphysical experiences or out-of-body experiences and be able to sense the etheric energies of the planet around you and the etheric energies of other human beings, animals, plants, and objects. By the way, the etheric-physical dimensions, the less dense part of the physical dimension, are a vast world, larger than the dense physical part.

Also on the etheric-physical dimension are the elemental spirits—real entities who live within the elements of Fire, Earth, Water and Air. There are many clairvoyant people who can see into the etheric dimension of the world, and it is quite common in psychic races like the Scottish and the Irish, who can see earth gnomes, air sylphs and other elemental creatures dancing in the waves or in fire. If you encounter etheric entities or etheric phenomena during your meditation sessions you have to be able to put your experiences in the right context; otherwise, you may become deluded and imagine that you are a prophet or something and do all kinds of strange things, which many people do.

Many naturally clairvoyant people become healers because they can see the auras around people; that is, they can see if there is anything wrong with the physical body by seeing into the etheric-physical body. What we call psychic healing is really etheric healing. The healer can sense the condition of your etheric body and can tell where your physical body is malfunctioning. Unfortunately, many psychic healers try to heal you by using their own etheric energy, which is a problem because their energies could be warped. When their warped energies enter your body the side effects can be much worse than the original problem before the healing. Just because people think they are healers because they feel energies through their hands or whatever, it doesn't necessarily mean that they are good healers; their own personal mechanism might not be pure, that is, it may not have a high-frequency vibration.

The next Centre is YESOD/the Foundation, which represents the Astral World (the astral body of planet Earth). The Astral World, like all the other worlds, has seven layers or dimensions, and it is divided into the lower Astral World, the middle Astral World and the higher Astral World. The Astral World is bigger than the Physical World (including the etheric-physical dimensions), extending from the centre of the planet (the lower Astral World) to about halfway to the moon (the higher Astral World). In other words, the denser the vibration of the Astral World, the closer it is to the centre of the Earth; and the more refined the vibration, the further away it is from the surface of the Earth.

The lower Astral World is the home of the negative spirits, which can be human, elemental or angelic spirits. It is also the home of what we call the hell worlds—hot hells, cold hells and other kinds of hells, a few of which I have been to. To be able to teach the Tree of Life, you have to experience "the things that are" because the Tree of Life is not a theoretical science or philosophy; it represents how things actually are. So I had to go to the hell worlds, and I'll tell you about one of them which is particularly interesting.

I can imagine that if a person has no idea about the Tree of Life and suddenly experiences this particular hell world, it would be a terrifying experience. You are in a dark space and can't see or hear anything, and you have a tremendous sense of being squashed and there is nothing you can do about it. You feel that something evil is about to pounce on you or crush you, or that something terrible is about to happen to you. The feeling is so strong that you cannot work out rationally what is happening. You are just in a dark space with an ominous feeling that something is going to annihilate you.

If you experience such a hell world, it feels like you have been there for eternity because in those worlds there is no sense of time. This is why religions say that if you go to Hell it will be for all eternity. That is true *when you are experiencing it*, because at that moment your consciousness is suspending the sensation of time, so the experience seems to go on forever, even if it lasted only one minute. Once you experience one of the hell worlds you can see why religions say that Hell is very bad and why they encourage you to be good.

The middle part of the Astral World, the third and fourth dimensions, is where the average person goes when they are dreaming during sleep, and when they cast off their body at death. Many spirits of the dead who communicate through mediums are from the middle part of the Astral.

When you are in the Astral World, you see everything that is in the Physical World, but the astral counterpart, which looks exactly the same except that it is made out of astral substance. If you are so-called dead, no longer in your physical body, and you go back to a place you knew on the Physical, you think that you are physically there because you see the identical astral counterpart of everything. If you are not instructed by a Teacher that you no longer have a physical body and what you are seeing is only the astral counterpart, you will believe that you are physically alive and are participating in the Physical World. Often, it takes people a long time to realize that they are actually dead.

But besides astral counterparts of physical things, the Astral World also has real astral entities and astral objects that are not based in the Physical World. There are astral cities and temples and astral groups that have no physical counterparts. Part of the delusion of the channellers and mediums is precisely that they feel that they are in a different world, or they are on a different planet, because the Astral World is so large and there are different sections in it.

When you go to the highest levels of the Astral World, the fifth, sixth and seventh dimensions, what we call the Astral Heavens, it is much brighter and quite beautiful in some places. The people there can look somewhat like angels, and they might even believe themselves to be special or from another planet, although they are actually still within the astral globe. It is quite common for Christians, if they see a shining being on the Astral, to think that it is Jesus or even God, and they will talk to that shining being believing that God is really talking to them. This is why there are many so-called communications from the Christ or the Buddha or some angelic being; deluded psychics think that they are really talking to those beings.

The whole industry of channelling and mediumship is based on Astral World phenomena, and sometimes some reasonably intelligent channelled material comes from the higher dimensions. But that, too, is only astral; it does not tell you the true picture at all. You cannot know the difference between the real and the unreal unless you have been taught to distinguish between what is simply an astral consciousness and what is a higher consciousness. One way to tell is that on the Astral World everything exists as a form, so if you see an embodied form, even a beautiful, shining angelic form, then you know you are still on the Astral World.

When people meditate and have internal experiences, problems can arise when they open themselves up to the Astral World without any knowledge of the Tree of Life. They do not know what level they are at and think that whatever they experience on the Astral is the highest possible experience, or that they have attained as far as human beings can go. This is why the Astral World is called the World of Delusion.

When you go beyond the Astral World, you enter the lower Mental World (NETZACH and HOD), which is bigger than the Astral World and extends well beyond the moon. This means that when you are on the Mental World you can travel in your mental body to the moon. On the Astral World you can travel to the moon only when the moon and the Earth reach their closest point, which is at the full moon period, when the astral body of the moon and the astral body of the Earth meet. The mental body of the planet (the Mental World) extends almost to Mars, so in your mental body you can travel to Mars when Mars is close.

Another important thing to know on your Inner Journey is that the Mental World is also made out of forms: beautiful geometric shapes like crosses, stars and complex geometric patterns; crystalline, translucent and exquisitely beautiful forms. If you see such a form while meditating, you will know that you are on the Mental World. On the Mental World you can travel to beautiful cities and meet highly intelligent beings and have many amazing experiences.

The next Centre on the Tree of Life is the Causal World (TIPHARETH/Beauty), which is the world of the Soul, the higher dimensions of the Mental World. But there is a tricky region between the Soul World and the lower Mental World. This is where the yogis and the Zen and Buddhist followers become stuck, because they reach a point in the meditation process where there is a mixture of mental activity and Pure Awareness. In other words, the Pure Awareness of the Soul is mingled with the consciousness of the mind, which is why the Buddhists are so intellectual. They try to somehow experience the Transcendental Consciousness—which is a no-mind experience—through the mind. They have not quite made it to the higher level of the Soul and are still locked into the mind level, so it can take them some time to sort out what is mind activity and what is Soul-Consciousness, or Pure Awareness.

When you are conscious of yourself as the Soul, you know that you are your Self *without mind.* While meditating, you suddenly feel timeless and spaceless, no longer connected to the idea of a physical body. This is when you begin to experience Pure Consciousness itself. However, this is only the middle part of the Tree of Life and the important thing is that from that point on (above the middle region of Tiphareth) *there are no forms*—the Tree of Life is formless. By this we mean that the upper part of the Tree of Life has to do with another kind of reality. For example, the region between TIPHARETH and DAATH is Pure Energy, Pure Consciousness, Pure Light, Pure Love, Pure Bliss, Pure Joy, but not embodied in a form or structure.

This gives you a big clue regarding where you are at in your meditation or in your journey towards Liberation. If you see any kind of form you know that your experience is below the Soul level; if you just feel Consciousness itself without shape or form, you know you are at the Soul level; you have reached beyond the lower worlds and can function as the Soul.

Your Soul is an entity; it has its own structure. Although it is a composite of Light-Energy, Love energy, Wisdom, Consciousness, and so on, it is still a structured form of energies, not in the sense of having arms and legs but in the way the energy impulses function inside you. It still has the sense of *I*, although a much higher sense than your personality sense of *I*.

The journey of the Soul begins when you begin to sense the next Centre of the Tree of Life, DAATH/Gnosis, which is called the Divine Darkness. This is the stage where your Soul realizes that beyond the bright, beautiful, joyful Heaven Worlds on the Soul level, there is an abyss, a divine darkness. It is experienced as a totally empty space, a dark, divine space where there is nothing. You have no sense of being a body or having a mind; there is just boundless infinite, dark Space.

This is the real test of your Soul because if your Soul gets out of the way and totally surrenders, the Divine Darkness will burst and the Absolute Light will manifest within you.

Then, the Journey begins in the realm of Absolute Light. This is the White Brilliance at the top of the Tree of Life (KETHER/the Crown), which the Buddha called Nirvāṇa and Christ called the Kingdom of God, and which is a brilliant field of Light permeating the entire Tree of Life. And that brilliant Light will dispel the Divine Darkness until nothing remains but the absolute White Brilliance.

When you reach that level, you are technically a Buddha or a Christ, somebody who has completed the Journey. That realm of brilliance is what we call the *Permanence*, a Light that never came into being because it always was and that will never go out because it always is. It is an endless Ocean of Light and all the beings in it are "sparks" of that Light, but not distinguishable from each other. When you are in Nirvāṇa, nevertheless, you know others individually; that is, in that Ocean of Light every particle of Light has its own separate reality although it is one with the Ocean.

According to Buddhism, when you go to Nirvāṇa you get annihilated, which is a hundred percent wrong, because in actual fact you don't get annihilated at all. What happens is that "you" as that spark simply become part of that infinite Ocean of Light. This does not mean that you lose your sense of *I-am-ness*. It is just that your sense of *I-am-ness* expands to infinity and you become that vast Ocean of Light.

As you move up the Tree of Life you will have some of the experiences I have described, and until you face the White Brilliance and merge into that Light, you will know that you still have a long way to go.

PRACTICE

Ruah: the Breath of Life

Ruah, the Breath of Life, is in every part of the Tree of Life. In the Physical World (Malkuth), your physical body is breathing air full of Prāṇa, energy from the Sun. That is Ruah on the physical level. In the etheric-physical dimensions, your etheric body is breathing in and out the etheric aura of Mother Earth, which is also Ruah. Further up the Tree of Life, in the Astral World (Yesod), your astral body is breathing in and out, and all the evolving lifeforms in the Astral World—human, subhuman and superhuman—rhythmically breathe in and out the life-force, Ruah.

In the Mind Worlds—the lower form worlds (Hod and Netzach) and higher formless worlds (Tiphareth)—all the entities, whichever Kingdom they belong to, breathe in and out the Life-Breath. And all the way up the Tree of Life to the level of Gnosis and beyond, to the first, second and third degrees of Enlightenment, every entity in the whole Tree of Life uses the Breath of Life, the Breath of God—Ruah.

The actual practice is quite simple: Sit in a comfortable chair or in your favourite meditation position and just focus on your breathing for a while. Then, as you breathe in say "RU" and as you breathe out say "AH". So, RU ... AH ... RU ... AH ....

RU ... AH

In ... Out

The word Ruah is a mantra, a magic word aligned to your breath current. In the beginning it is you, the little self, consciously breathing in "RU" and breathing out "AH", more aware of the mantra than your own breath. But eventually there comes a moment when the mantra fades into a fine vibration and you suddenly realize that you are not breathing at all, that something else is breathing inside you: the subtle breath, the etheric breath. Then, as you progress in this breathing meditation you start to slowly climb up the Tree of Life, breathing in your astral body and then in your mental body. When you reach the Soul level, you realize that it is the *Soul* that is breathing inside you, that it is the Soul's life-force that is maintaining you, keeping your whole personality mechanism going.

As you go further in this breath meditation, however, there comes another realization: that the Soul itself is being breathed upon. You realize that the Soul is not the real cause but that further up there is a greater entity that is breathing upon your Soul, keeping your Soul alive. The *Spirit*, on the level of Gnosis, is breathing and keeping the billions of Souls in the Causal World alive. When you reach KETHER, the Crown, you realize that in fact *the only thing that is breathing is the Spirit of God.* From the lowest to the highest, everywhere through all Time and Space, it is the Spirit of God that is breathing in and out, maintaining everything in Manifestation.

Then comes the final realization:

The Spirit of God Is Breathing within You.

When you realize that it is not you who is breathing but the Spirit of God, you will *know* that you and God are One, and you will be in the state of Absolute Enlightenment and will have fulfilled God's plan and purpose for your Natural and Supernatural Evolution.

The Nine Pillars of Wisdom of the Mystery School

A Mystery School is based on nine pillars, the *Nine Pillars of Wisdom*, which are symbolic of the qualities that a true Mystery School must have. The first three pillars are obvious, the next three are less obvious and the last three are quite subtle.

1. Focus and Concentration on the Spiritual Path

The first pillar of a Mystery School is focus and concentration on the Spiritual Path. Many spiritual schools are more like communes, focused on being vegetarian, growing their own food, exercising and tuning into Nature, and they do not have a strong spiritual focus. A true Spiritual School is focused on the Spiritual Path and it does not get sidetracked, for example, into the details of communal living. To live as a commune is fine, but a commune is never going to be a proper Mystery School or a proper Ashram.

2. The Memory of the Eternal Law

The basis of a Mystery School is that there is an ancient, undying Reality, the Law of the Universe, which was called TORAH in the ancient Hebrew Mystery Schools and SANĀTANA-DHARMA in the Hindu and Buddhist Ashrams.[16] The Memory of the Eternal Law means that in

16. Nowadays, of course, the worldly-minded people misinterpret those words: TORAH is understood as the laws, rules and regulations that the Rabbis invented, and SANĀTANA-DHARMA is used to refer to the orthodox Hindu religion.

the background of the Mystery School there is an understanding that there exists a vast, unbounded Cosmic Reality that is eternal, unchanging and absolute, regardless of time and space conditions. In other words, there is a Law in the Universe that orders and keeps together all the vast systems of Creation (worlds upon worlds, realms upon realms, universes upon universes) and that is guarded by hidden Spiritual Laws. The memory of that Law is always present and the whole teaching of the Mystery School is based on it. Without the Memory of the Eternal Law there is no school.

3. *Creative Imagination to Present the Truth in the Time and Place Situation*

All the founders of true Mystery Schools were enlightened people who lived by the Eternal Law and had an understanding of the Cosmos and human beings, but they had to have *imagination* to present the Truth according to the time and place they were in. Obviously, societies in India, Greece, Rome, Egypt and China were different according to time and place; therefore, the enlightened Masters of the schools had to use their imagination to adapt their knowledge of the Truth to the people they were teaching.

Christ had to speak a simple language because He was not talking to learned people but to fishermen and farmers. He always talked about simple household things that people could understand and never used metaphysical words. Buddha, however, used metaphysical language because He was talking to the learned, intellectual Brahmins and Vedic scholars of the day.

What we are trying to say is that the fundamental Truth is always the same, regardless of country, time and place, but the Teacher has to tune into the local culture, language and situation and use imagination to teach the Eternal Truth in a way that suits the people he or she is talking to.

4. *Reasonable and Logical Explanation of the Truth*

The way to communicate Truth to people is to present it in a rational and reasonable way so that they understand it on their own terms. This is why Christ used a simple language, with references to sheep, farming, treasures in fields and all sorts of things that people could relate to. This is where Zen is a failure in terms of explaining the spiritual mysteries because it uses a lot of clever words and riddles that people do not really understand. The Truth can be explained rationally and reasonably, and this is fundamental to the Teaching of a Mystery School.

5. *The Need for a Spiritual Teacher*

In the sixties and seventies new-agers and hippies established ashrams and communes in countries around the world. They would buy a piece of land, put up a building and say that they had an ashram. At the time I looked at a few of them and pointed out that they had the buildings and the land, but there was one problem: there was no Guru or Teacher; there was no *connection* to the Higher Reality, no Pillar of Light. When Jesus spoke, He was called a Rabbi because people understood that He was an enlightened Master, not because He belonged to a particular sect of the Jewish religion.

A Mystery School needs an enlightened Teacher, and if it does not have one it is unable to function, because it is through the Teacher that the whole Mystery School system works.

6. *Togetherness, Cooperation and Companionship*

Those who come to a Mystery School must have a sense of togetherness, cooperation and companionship among themselves. In the olden days, this was very real: the bond with members of the School was stronger than the natural physical bond with relatives, even with mothers, fathers or children. A person in a Mystery School was happy to sacrifice everything, even die, for another person in the School. When Christ said, "No man has greater love than he who sacrifices his life for another man" *(John* 15:13), He was talking about the pupils in His School.

In those days, the members of a Mystery School had a Soul bonding that was eternal, beyond space and time, but nowadays this is not understood because of the ego-centredness of the modern generation. A modern Mystery School must have this strong bonding and cooperation among members because they understand the enormous task the School has and the vision behind it, and they know that they need to sacrifice their life for that goal.

7. *Receptivity to Higher Energies*

This is the first of the more subtle pillars. As a member of a Mystery School you have to not just listen with your physical ears but to *feel* beyond the words that there are other processes, other methods of instruction and communication, taking place. And to register them you have to develop receptivity to higher energies. If everyone is just listening with their ears and their minds, nothing much can be achieved and little can happen to them because they are blocking the energies. The more the members of the School can develop this receptivity and feel the higher energies at work, the more the work of the School can be done.

8. *The Employment of Dynamic Techniques to Invoke Higher Energies*

In our Mystery School we use Mantra, sacred symbols, chanting, meditation, intonation, visualization—all dynamic techniques that invoke higher energies. In a true Mystery School you cannot just give knowledge; you need to have dynamic techniques because you actually have to *invoke* the Higher Reality into manifestation. Then, you can *work* with the higher energies, which is the last pillar of the Mystery School.

9. *Working with the Forces of Light*

The last pillar is the most hidden. Working with the Forces of Light is a subtle work in which we try to create links with the Kingdom of God.

So the Nine Pillars of Wisdom explain what the true Mystery Schools were, in all times and all places, and they apply to any future Mystery School. Normally, the word *mystery* means something that cannot be understood, something irrational or illogical, but the original meaning of the word as it is used in *Mystery School* means something that *can be unveiled or revealed.* And that is what happens in our Mystery School: the mysteries are revealed and the members are enlightened a bit more every day so that they will see the Infinite Knowledge-Field that is possible if they are ready for it.

Faith-based Systems and Knowledge-based Systems

Many people do not know that there are differences between faith-based systems and knowledge-based systems in terms of spirituality. Typical faith-based systems are Christian Mysticism, Muslim Sūfīsm, Zen and, for the most part, the Indian Ashram system. They are based on faith, a belief in the possibility of Liberation—or Union with God, Self-Realization or whatever they want to call it—but the followers are not given the direct knowledge involved to become liberated.

The Christian Mystics, for example, had tremendous faith and did everything they could for their faith, meditating and having all kinds of experiences, but they didn't really know what they were doing. It was the same with the Prophets of ancient Israel: they spent years meditating in the desert, invoking the Divine Name, but nobody gave them the precise knowledge of what to do, why they should do it and what results to expect. Zen has no esoteric knowledge, just a belief that something will happen if you meditate. And most Indian ashrams are based on faith that the Guru is a living God or an incarnation of God and he or she will save you.

Now, the ancient Mystery Schools were different: they were knowledge-based. They knew precisely what had to be done, why, how and when, and what sequence of actions had to be followed. In other words, their teachers had *Inner Knowledge*—Gnosis, Wisdom, Understanding—gained by direct experience because they were esoteric teachers, not ordinary religious teachers or priests. They did not just have faith but actual experience. This is the difference between all the many systems of spirituality that are based on faith and those that have a precise system with teachers who have accumulated real wisdom through experience.

So a Mystery School like ours is based on knowledge. We understand every part of the process from beginning to end: all the detailed knowledge of the Inner Worlds of Creation, where human beings fit in, what the goal of Humanity is, and so on. There is nothing based on faith or belief. Many people come into our School from a faith-based system and expect everything to be simple, just receive a mantra and then be saved. That is how it would be in a faith-based system, but the Spiritual Path does not work like that.

For instance, I knew of a lady who followed an Indian Guru for many years. She believed that he was an incarnation of God and would save her, but after thirty years nothing had happened. So one day she said to the Guru that she had been doing what he had told her to do for thirty years but nothing had happened. Of course, he had no answer because in a faith-based system the idea is that you believe in the possibility that you will get there, but no one can tell you precisely *why* you do not get there.

In a true Mystery School you are told what you have to do from day one. The Teacher knows what obstacles and problems you have to face, what you have to do to overcome them, and why something does or does not work. That is why it is important to follow the instructions, as well as the rules and regulations, because they are based on experience. It is like when Moses gave the Ten Commandments or Buddha gave the Four Noble Truths or Christ gave the Beatitudes: they didn't make them up because that is what they believed. The Masters *knew* that if people want to make the transition from "here" to "there", they have to do certain things so that they can change themselves enough to receive the Inner Revelation. You cannot just be a normal person and get there; it's just not possible.

The Levels of the Mystery School

The Mystery School has layers, or levels, of working. It has a physical structure—it has buildings—but it is not just physical. It is not like a university or a school where you study some subjects and then graduate and leave because there's nothing more beyond that. The Mystery School extends into the Astral World and then goes further up into the mind dimensions, where you are given knowledge—lower knowledge through your rational mind and higher knowledge through your intuitional mind.

But the Mystery School extends beyond the mind dimensions into the Buddhic dimensions, the World of Unity, whose symbol is the Sacred Flame in the Inner Sanctuary of the Mystery School. If you progress through the School to the Buddhic World, you are what in the Indian system is called a Self-Realized person—a great Yogī, a Guru, an Adept or a Master; you have become One with the All, you have reached the highest form of Yoga. People who reach the Sacred Fire and merge into it think that they have reached the final goal, the Final Reality, that there is no further to go.

However, the Mystery School goes beyond the Indian system, beyond all the faith-based schools, because it extends to NIRVĀṆA, which Buddha attained during His lifetime, and PARANIRVĀṆA, Buddha's final attainment. (Above that is what we call the Plane of ĀDI, the Primordial Fire, the Original Source of the Cosmos.) Once you have graduated to the level of Nirvāṇa, you have entered into the Kingdom of God, which is beyond the normal human attainment. At that point your supernatural, nonhuman evolution—your divine evolution—begins. If you still have your physical body at that time you will still appear in your normal physical body in the physical world. But on the Soul level you will be completely reoriented, reorganized and reformed into another being, a being that is able to function in the Nirvāṇic dimensions.

So the Mystery School is a multidimensional reality that stretches all the way from the physical dimension to beyond Nirvāṇa. How far you get, of course, depends on your level of understanding and what you do.

People in the faith-based systems do not realize that merely believing in God or believing in the Guru or believing in something is a good start but it doesn't mean that you should sit around on your backside and do nothing after that. There are many Teachers in the world, especially Hindu Swamis, who say, "Come and sit at my feet and you will be liberated." It's an easy trap to fall into and many people go to them and sit at their feet, listen to what they say and think they are liberated. But they are miles away from Liberation. Yes, the Teacher is necessary, but that does not mean that you sit back and do nothing. The Teacher only gives you certain possibilities. If you don't actually *do something yourself*—the right thing—you won't get there.

Why do you think that the Christ said that many are called but few are chosen? There are over one billion Christians in the world, and how many of them are in the Kingdom of God? There are over one billion Muslims. How many of them are in the Kingdom of God? There are a few hundred million Buddhists. How many of them are in Nirvāṇa? Many are called (many believe in God, Buddha or Christ) but few are chosen (few reach their spiritual destination).

The ancient Mystery Schools had an outer court, an inner court and a sanctuary. Many were called and came in through the gate and entered the outer court. They listened to what the Teacher had to say and they stayed there. So long as they did not do the right thing they never got to the next court, much less the sanctuary.

To reach the Sacred Flame in the Sanctuary (the Buddhic World), you have to undergo some tests, and the *Guardian of the Sacred Flame* is there to make sure that you don't get through unless you have passed them.

The Four Tests of the Mystery School

Esoteric Schools such as the Freemasons, Rosicrucians, Alchemists and Kabbalists always talk about mysterious tests you have to go through, and about initiation by water, initiation by fire, initiation by air, initiation by earth. (In the Esoteric School system they are called *initiations*, but they are actually tests.) People think that these are just nice ideas that have nothing to do with reality, but before you can approach the Inner Sanctuary you have to go through four tests, and there is no escaping that. The first is the Test of Earth.

1. *The Test of Earth: wealth, ego, pride, fame, name, attachment*

There is a story in the New Testament about a rich young man who came to Jesus and said, "Master, what can I do to attain the kingdom of God?" (*Matthew* 19: 16). Jesus said, "Sell all your goods and follow me" (*Matthew* 19: 21). Very simple. The young man was shocked and went home and did nothing. Why? Because he liked his wealth, fame and name and he could not give them up. He failed the Test of Earth.

This does not mean that you cannot have money, that you have to be miserable and poor like a sadhu and give everything up. But what is your relationship to Earth, this world? If you are attached to your name and fame, then you stay on the level of Earth. This is the biggest test for many people, especially those who are "successful" in the world, who expect everybody to honour them just because they are good in music, sports, acting or something or another. There is nothing wrong with the actual attainment itself and there is nothing wrong with being rich, but if your attainment or riches prevent you from moving on spiritually, then you have to rethink how you relate to things.

In ancient times in India, for instance, during the Vedic civilization six thousand years ago, most of the kings of India were Yogīs, great masters of Yoga. It was the same with King Solomon and King David. They were powerful and rich but they were primarily God-oriented and spiritual. And so were the early pharaohs that ruled ancient Egypt and the kings of ancient China and Japan. This means that you can be rich and famous and still enter the Inner Sanctuary. It's your *attitude* that counts.

Many people fail the Test of Earth because they are stingy. They don't want to pay for things; they want to keep their money for themselves. They do not realize that the only way things can be maintained in the physical world is with money. It's the commonly agreed exchange system. (In fact, it's the one thing the whole planet has agreed on. You realize how amazing that is! Otherwise nobody agrees on anything, as you know.) So money is the most practical way to maintain the physical order of things, and what you do with your money determines whether or not you pass the Test of Earth.

2. *The Test of Water: emotions, feelings, moods, tantrums*

Whereas the Test of Earth is related to the Physical Plane, the Test of Water relates to the Astral Plane, which means you are also tested on your emotions and moods. The Test of Water is real, and to pass it you have to watch your emotions and moods all the time because if they are warped, that is to say, you are continually in a bad mood, the Guardian will stop you going any further, even if you pass the Test of Earth.

It is also important to do your job, your service, gladly, because you understand that it is necessary for the existence of the school you belong to. In Indian Ashrams everybody does something: somebody looks after the garden, somebody sweeps the floors, somebody does the cooking. In the West people complain because they have to do a few chores. They throw a tantrum, so they do not pass the test. It's very simple.

3. *The Test of Air: thoughts, life-force (Prāṇa)*

The life-force within you, or Prāṇa, is aligned with your mind; whatever you think affects your Prāṇa. If you are afraid, for example, the thought of fear stops your breathing immediately. So the Test of Air is important because every thought affects your life-breath, which affects your physical body and your whole environment. If you are continually thinking materialistically, if you are self-centred and negative, you won't go beyond the Thought World and therefore cannot get anywhere near the Sanctuary.

The ancient Sages made rules that were based on facts: that progress in spiritual life depends on certain things that you have to do. Everybody agrees that there should be tests to determine if students of regular schools and universities are to pass or not, but in spiritual life people resent the idea that they have to be tested. Everybody wants to become a Buddha or a Christ after the first lesson. If you think like that, you will fail the Test of Air.

4. *The Test of Fire: Spiritual strength or inspiration*

The last one, the Test of Fire, is the most difficult. It's a test of how sincere you are about your spiritual life. Are you lukewarm or are you really full on? If you say, "She'll be alright, I'll get there some time." Well, that's true: you will get there sometime, but not in this lifetime. So the Test of Fire is about your internal burning, what in India is called TAPAS and what in the West is called Zeal, the burning motive power inside you. The Guardian of the Sacred Flame will reject anybody who is not zealous. That's how it is and that's how it should be.

PRACTICE

(1)

IAŌ-AIŌ Invocation

This particular technique awakens the Head Centres, which consist of the Third-Eye Chakra, the Crown Chakra, and the minor chakra at the back of the neck. The Head Centres form a triangle and intoning and meditating on IAŌ-AIŌ will stimulate and awaken these three Head Centres simultaneously.

This way of intoning does not use a particular note. The vowels are first intoned separately and then joined together to form the proper mantra. You always have to do the individual sounds first so that they become established, and then you glide the vowels together to intone the mantra. This is according to the Greek Mystery School way of working with this particular type of mantra, which is an ancient Divine Name.

Now, start by putting your attention in your total head area, not one of the individual Head Centres. Then intone IAŌ-AIŌ aloud a few times, first with the vowels separated and then with the vowels joined together.[17] Then mentally intone IAŌ-AIŌ with the vowels glided together for about ten minutes. And then let your mind be completely still and do nothing and just wait for an after-effect. You don't have to produce anything and it doesn't matter what happens or whether you perceive an after-effect or not. Just sit still and keep your mind still. That's all you have to do.

17. An audio file demonstrating the correct intonation of this mantra, both the separate and glided forms, can be found at www.planetary-transformation.org/mantrarepetition. The separate form can be used for the intonation that is part of the meditation exercise on the following page.

PRACTICE

(2)

IAŌ-AIŌ Invocation & Meditation

IAŌ-AIŌ is a mantric formula meaning "I am invoking the Guiding Light." A mantra does not have to have a meaning but it has one in terms of its Sound structure producing certain effects. And the effect of IAŌ-AIŌ is that the Guiding Light, which comes from the Soul level, the Causal World, comes to you because you invoke it.

If you don't invoke the Light, it does not come to you. Many Westerners do not understand the ancient spiritual truths or rules that have been taught for thousands of years, mainly because they are too materialistic. For example, you may have heard of the *Quest for the Holy Grail.* The legend of King Arthur is just one of many legends of knights from France, Italy, Germany and other parts of Europe going on quests for the Holy Grail. *Grail* is an old English word for "cup" and the knights were looking for the cup that Jesus used at the Last Supper or the cup that contained the Water of Immortality. They did not know that the Holy Grail is the Light of the Higher Mind dimensions, and that the *quest* has nothing to do with going around the country looking for a cup.

The quest is about invoking the Light, which means you are actively seeking it, actively doing something about it. The Light is there—it is everywhere—but you have to invoke it. If you do not invoke the Light, you will not connect to it. You have to make a conscious connection to it and the mantric formula IAŌ-AIŌ will help you to do that. When you intone it and think, "I am invoking the Guiding Light," you will begin to become aware of the Light because you are acknowledging that the Light is there, and it will respond.

First you are going to stand up and intone IAŌ-AIŌ loudly and clearly, and as you intone the mantra, you think, "I am invoking the Guiding Light." Then, after you have intoned the mantra physically, aloud, you will sit down and intone it silently in your mind, intoning IAŌ-AIŌ and at that same time holding the thought "I am invoking the Guiding Light" in your mind. So there are two things happening: you are resonating the sound in your mind and at the same time your mind is focused on the idea that you are invoking the Light.

Remember, the key to it is that you are making the sound internally and at the same time you are *willing* the Light to come to you. Then, sit down in a comfortable position and close your eyes and focus in the Head Centre, not on the Third-Eye Chakra but the whole head region. Intone IAŌ-AIŌ mentally, precisely and clearly, and at the same time think of the downpour of Light. Do that for about ten minutes and then remain in silence.

The Mystery School and Phenomena

Many Indian Yogīs are into phenomena, or what they call SIDDHIS, "magical powers". For example, Sai Baba used to materialize objects and Hindu religious symbols such as sacred ash and jewellery. Tibetan Yogīs and Saints, or TULKU, spent lifetimes developing magical powers like walking on water or fire and levitating into the air. In India, if someone demonstrates the slightest phenomena, like emanating a perfume, levitating or other Yogic power, they are declared an incarnation of God or an Avatāra. In Tibet they do the same thing but the Tibetans don't call them Avatāras, just accomplished Yogīs or people who have magical powers.

Nowadays in the West people don't believe in magical powers because it's not scientific to believe in such things. Scientific materialism says that people with such powers are hallucinating or are mentally ill. But in reality they are not psychotic or mad; they are actually working on different levels than what the scientists work on. I'm not saying that these powers are good for them, but the point is, they exist.

Another important point is that most pupils when they begin any Spiritual Path, whether it is the system of Yoga, Zen, Sūfism, Buddhism, Mysticism, Kabbalah or whatever, identify spiritual progress with phenomena. They have a tendency to expect something to happen to them, to see flashing lights or hear sounds when they are meditating, and if such phenomena do not occur they think they are not making any progress. This is a common mistake.

In our Mystery School we come from a high level of Consciousness and have an understanding of the various degrees of phenomena. So we teach how to rightly understand phenomena: where they come from, what level of activity they show, their usefulness—and in particular how they can completely hinder your spiritual progress.

Power is called SIDDHI in Yogic literature, ŚAKTI in India and SHEKINAH in the West. But the English word *power* (or its equivalent in other modern languages) does not convey the real meaning of those words. When people hear the word *power* they think of electric power or motive power, but the actual meaning of Siddhi, Shekinah or Śakti—Power—is way beyond that. It's an omnific power of various grades that can move Heaven and Earth. We have to use a standard, but understand that the word *Power* here doesn't mean something that humans have made. When you understand what Power is, you will be able to put every experience in the right context.

So we'll start with this basic fact: Power exists. So what is Power? It is the Deity Himself or Herself. In terms of Śakti and Shekinah it's feminine, or you could say the Goddess Power, and in terms of Siddhi it's masculine. In the Absolute State, of course, Power is neither masculine nor feminine. The following will give you a better understanding of what Power is and how it manifests in Creation.

Power Level I

The Primary Yogic Power: Divine Power (above the Soul Level)

We will start at the very top: Power as expressed on the divine level, or the higher levels of the Tree of Life. That is the first manifestation of Power, which is above the Soul level. This power is:

The Power of Pure Consciousness Without Embodiment.

The Power of Pure Consciousness without embodiment can only be experienced above the level of your Soul. On that level there are no planets, no stars, no suns, no human beings—nothing, just Consciousness itself—absolute, boundless, timeless; the Source of Reality; the No-Thing, before anything happened to limit Consciousness.

And the First Power, Divine Power, is:

Omniscience, Omnipresence and Omnipotence.

Obviously, to experience this level of Power, the Divine Power, you have to be so developed in your spiritual life that you can touch layers of experience above your Soul. It is the kind of experience the Buddha or the Christ would have, or great Master Yogīs, Sūfīs or Saints, people who attained the highest possible human development and went beyond and merged with what we call the Fifth Kingdom or the Spiritual Hierarchy. This is the Enlightened Consciousness, Enlightenment or Illumination.

When your internal development goes beyond the level of your Soul, in that field of unlimited Consciousness, there is nothing but Absolute Awareness, which gives you the sensation of omniscience, omnipresence and omnipotence.

Omnipotence means you feel that you can do anything, you can manifest anything, you can become anything, you can create a whole universe. (The Buddhists say that those who reach Buddhahood can create a universe, which they call a *Buddha-field*.)

Omnipresence means you feel that you are everywhere, in every universe, in every condition; that you can manifest yourself on this Earth or in the Sun or in the next Solar System.

Omniscience means you *know*; you know everything that is needed to be known. It doesn't mean that you know the contents of an encyclopaedia. It's not intellectual knowledge. Omniscience is a state of *being* that is everywhere simultaneously, that knows everything all at once. It is not something you can attain through your mind because it is three levels above the mind.

The Divine Power is the Object of Attainment of the Mystery School.

The objective of the Mystery School is to get you to that state, or give you a vision of the possibility of rising out of your bodily consciousness, going through the astral consciousness and the intellectual regions of the mind, including the Higher Mind, and going to the region of Gnosis (DAATH) on the Tree of Life, and even above that. That was the high objective of the great Mystery Schools of Egypt, Rome, Greece, China and India: to take you to the very top of the Tree of Life.

Power Level II

The Secondary Yogic Powers: The Powers of the Soul

When you become Soul-Conscious you reach the level where you can understand things beyond the mind, where you no longer use the mind to understand. When you reach that level you have what we call the secondary Yogic Powers, the Powers of the Soul. Sai Baba and other Indian Yogīs who have attained Soul-Consciousness manifest Soul Powers. They don't have to, but they do because they want to. If you do that then you have already lost your way: you do not go further up the Spiritual Path. And you will see why.

When you reach Soul-Consciousness, the danger is that you start displaying those powers and then everybody worships you as a great Saint or Avatāra (which happens in India all the time) and you enjoy it. Then, you develop another ego besides your personal ego—what we call the spiritual ego—which enjoys all the attention you receive, and that immediately cuts you off from moving further up the Path. That is why all the true Spiritual Schools and the true Gurus tell you to *leave Power alone!* So what are these powers of the Soul?

1. The Power to See Minute Things

One of the Yogic Powers you can have when you are Soul-Conscious and have developed your Soul mechanism is that you are able to look into things and see on a very small scale. You can look into your body, for instance, and you can tell if any of the cells are not functioning properly. Those with this power can know when a particular group of cells is going to cause cancer or some other disease. They can focus inside things so minutely that they can see bacteria or even atoms and find out how things are internally structured.

2. *The Power to See Large Things*

When this power of the Soul is developed you are able to see the whole planet simultaneously. You can see what is happening on the other side of the planet, if there is an earthquake or a volcano erupting somewhere, and you can describe what is happening. In other words, the capacity of the Soul has expanded to embrace the planet, and when that power is developed further it can even embrace the whole Solar System so that you see the planets and how they move.

As I said, the tragedy is that once you start getting hooked by Power you get locked into a "power trip". You forget the Spiritual Path; you forget to move up into the realms of Pure Consciousness.

3. *The Power of Stability*

If you develop the power of stability, nothing will shake you or move you. And this is physically so. Yogīs with this power can sit in the lotus posture or stand up and root themselves firmly to the ground so that nobody can move them. Half a dozen people can try to move them but they won't be able to, no matter what they do. This is the physical expression of this power, but what it really means is that the Soul within you is so stable that nothing happening in the world can disturb you. Even if an atomic bomb explodes next to you it makes no difference to you. Your physical body will disappear, but your internal structure will not change or move at all. (Remember, this is a Soul Power, like all the Yogic Powers; you have to associate them with the Soul, not your personality.) Such inner stability can be a useful quality—it can help you weather the storms of life—but like the other powers it can obstruct your spiritual development if it is overused.

4. *The Power of Levitation*

The ability to levitate is a common and popular power among the Hindu Yogīs. Levitation means overcoming gravity and there are two kinds of levitation: one which is willed and one that is only possible if you are holy. You can purposefully levitate because after many years of meditation you can learn to focus your attention in the Causal Centre and draw the energies up from your body in a stream until the rising energy stream becomes so powerful that you are physically lifted off the ground. You do not need to love God or even be on the Spiritual Path to do this, but this type of levitation is not the real thing.

The real levitation is that of the Christian, Jewish, Muslim and other Saints who levitate because of *devotion.* Their devotion towards God is so intense—and in their consciousness God is somewhere "up there" in Heaven—that they literally rise up towards the sky. This is the neutralization of gravity through pure devotion, which is very different and much more positive than simply wanting to develop the power to levitate.

5. *The Power to Attain: the All-Consuming Desire*

In Soul-Consciousness, you can have an all-consuming desire to become something, and you will attain it. A fire begins to burn inside you, the Fire of Desire, and it is so powerful that it will rearrange the world around you so that you will achieve what you desire. There is an interesting story about an Indian Guru who had an all-consuming desire from a past life to be a king and have a big palace and so on. His Master, who also had Yogic Powers, looked inside him and saw that this desire from past lives would stop him from going further up the Path. So the Master fulfilled the pupil's desire on the astral, mental and causal levels, and for a short time the Guru was the king and ruler of a country. Then the Master shattered that image, freeing him so he could move up the Path.

6. *Irresistible Willpower to Conquer*

Irresistible willpower means the ability to overcome anything. The great conquerors of history, the builders of the Persian, Roman and other empires, all had the irresistible willpower to conquer. Hitler had it, and Mussolini, Stalin and Alexander the Great had it. The only problem is that they misused it because they did not know how to move up to the next region of the Tree of Life.

7. *Creative Imagination to Materialize Objects*

This power is the ability to materialize objects. You establish yourself in Soul-Consciousness, which means you can get in touch with the Soul realms, the upper Causal Worlds, at will. Then, you visualize an object, like a flower, and keep focusing the Soul Power until the object condenses and literally appears in physical reality.

8. *Magical Power*

Magical power gives you control over humans, animals and subhuman species, which could mean anything from the Plant, Mineral and Elemental Kingdoms. This was popular in the Middle and the Dark Ages in the West, when magicians would invoke demons or lower elementals. Those magicians were not part of a Mystery School and did not know that this magical power would trap and ultimately destroy them. That's because the demons and entities they invoked would initially obey them but then subtly take control over them. So most of those magicians usually ended up insane.

This power is usually obtained through ritual because the ritual helps you to tune into your Soul-nature and derive the energy and power from there.

Power Level III

Psychic Power of the Personality

The third level of Power, psychic power, is part of the personality, and at the time of Atlantis it was normal for everybody to have psychic powers because the rational mind had not yet been developed in human beings; in other words, we didn't know how to *think* but had strong psychic abilities. Since the Atlantean continent stretched from North America to Great Britain, many psychics nowadays are from Britain, Canada and America because they are reincarnations of the old Atlanteans.

Although being psychic was the normal way of being at the time of Atlantis, it is not normal now because of our materialistic civilization. Materialistic education, with its focus on developing the rational mind, destroys any possibility of extrasensory experience; the more mental you are, the less possibility there is for you to express psychic power. Children are naturally born with psychic powers because of our Atlantean past, but as soon as they go to school and have so much information put into their young brains, their psychic ability is lost.

Still, some people are born with psychic powers and are able to retain them. The problem with natural-born psychics is that they tend to think that they are God Almighty, or Goddess Almighty, because they have clairvoyance or other psychic ability, and they do not want to hear that there are stages of development way above the level of psychic power. So they get trapped on their level of Power.

Remember that these are powers existing within the personality—we all have them—but they are not awakened. This is why you don't know that you have them. You can, however, awaken them: indirectly, through drugs or certain types of alcohol, or directly, through yogic and mediumistic practices. During the late nineteenth century, for example, the development of psychic powers was particularly popular in America. People went to séances and so-called *development circles*, where they worked on developing psychic powers, and they went to channellers and mediums, who can awaken psychic powers in others.

So what are these psychic powers?

1. *Telepathy (Thought Reading)*

Telepathy is thought reading, the ability to read somebody else's thoughts, feelings and moods. When you know what your spouse is thinking, that's telepathy. It is a natural ability if it is awakened, but often it is used unconsciously. That is because this power can be partially awakened depending on your particular circumstances, so you can sometimes pick up through your mind what somebody else is thinking, usually something about you or the situation you are in.

Telepathy is particularly important in the Spiritual Warrior School, because a Warrior has to be able to read the enemy's thoughts. Part of the Warrior training is learning to sense your opponent's thoughts, feelings, attitudes and vibrations, because that can save your life. When you are a Master Warrior you know precisely your opponent's next move. But remember, telepathy is still just a psychic power and has to do with your personality.

2. *Clairvoyance*

Clairvoyance is seeing into the etheric, astral and mental dimensions; specifically, with this faculty you can see the etheric part of the Physical World, the lower and higher parts of the Astral World and the lower part of the Mental World. When you see geometric patterns, like stars, squares, cubes or crosses, you are seeing the lower mental dimensions. Images of flowers, human beings and angelic or other kinds of beings come from the higher astral dimensions, whereas sensory phenomena are more likely to come from the lower astral levels.

A big problem for clairvoyants is that they believe that whatever they see has huge significance, that they have been specially selected to bring a big message to the world. In other words, their egos become inflated. Normally, the ego resides on the level of the mental dimensions, but for the clairvoyant the ego becomes centred on the astral level, so whatever happens on that level becomes all-important, even though it is mostly trivial, or even wrong.

3. *Clairsentience*

Another psychic ability of the personality is clairsentience, which means feeling or sensing invisible energies, places, people or objects. The police sometimes use psychics with this faculty. They give the psychic an item of clothing or an object that belonged to a missing person or the victim of a crime, and the clairsentient can sense the invisible energies emanating from that object and follow the energy pattern to wherever that person is, whether the person is dead or alive.

Sometimes ordinary people with some development of this power can also sense that something is wrong with a place or situation. You may be walking along a street in a big city and get a creepy sensation that you shouldn't go around a certain corner, so you turn around and go the other way. That's clairsentience. And this is another faculty that is an important part of the Spiritual Warrior training, because sensing invisible energies in places, people and objects can make a difference to the outcome of a battle.

4. *Past Impressions*

The term *past impressions* refers to past lifetimes—impressions of being in ancient Greece or Rome, or in ancient China or India—or the past of *this* lifetime. You may meet someone you've never met before and immediately get an impression that you have been with that person in the past. That is a past impression, another of the psychic senses of the personality.

5. *Premonitions: Sensing the Future*

The opposite of a past impression is a premonition, which is about sensing something that is going to happen in the future. Sometimes, when there is a major earthquake, airplane crash or other disaster, some psychics have premonitions of it a few days or months before.

Many years ago I had an impression that I was in a snowy village somewhere in Germany, walking alongside a little boy who was holding my hand. We were walking along a country road at the edge of the village, with houses and farmlands on each side. It was a very clear impression, visual as well as sensory; I could even feel the warmth of the child's hand in mine.

Years later, on my first trip to Europe, I was with my son and we ended up in Germany in a little village. Of course, I had never given any thought to that old premonition. We were staying a few days with friends in Germany, and it was winter, with lots of snow everywhere. One evening I went our for a walk with my son, who was about five years old at the time, and we walked down to the end of the village, when I noticed his warm little hand holding mine. Suddenly I looked around and was amazed. Everything I was seeing—the road, the houses, the farms—was exactly what I saw in my impression many years previously.

It may seem strange that you can sense something that is going to happen in the future, but it can be explained because the future exists on the higher mental dimensions, on the level of the Reincarnating Ego. Because the Reincarnating Ego (the Soul) has a plan for the future, you (the incarnated ego) can be in the physical world and use your psychic ability through your astral body and actually glimpse something that the Reincarnating Ego knows is going to take place. Then you have a premonition.

6. *Clairaudience: Hearing Within*

Clairaudience is the last of the personality powers, and it can be quite dangerous; it is the fall of many psychics. Clairaudience means that you hear voices, either the chatter of the Astral World or specific voices telling you things.

When a radio is tuned between stations, you can hear static noise and bits and pieces of one station or the other. In the same way, when you have the first type of a clairaudience, you can hear bits of the Astral World, noises here and there, people speaking about all kinds of things—the whole vibration of life of the Astral World.

With the other type of clairaudience, you hear entities telling you things. Often, people who have committed a violent crime or murder say that they were hearing voices that told them to do it. Many of these people are actually clairaudient and hear the voice of an astral entity that attaches itself to them and tells them to do things—sometimes good things, sometimes bad things. The problem is that if a clairaudient has not been trained in a proper spiritual school, he or she does not know the danger of the situation. Unfortunately, clairaudient people tend to believe whatever the voices tell them—usually that they have been chosen to save the world or something like that—and you cannot tell them otherwise. They won't believe you when you tell them that they are just ordinary people with a clairaudient faculty.

However, there is also a positive side to hearing within: you can get in touch with the voice of the Higher Self. Now, *that* voice is completely different than the voices coming from the Astral World. There is a simple way to know the difference between the voice of the Higher Self within you and what is just some astral entity telling you nonsense or misleading information. The real Voice will not tell you that you are the Christ, that you are special, that you have been chosen for a special mission. The real Voice will tell you to shape up! It will tell you that unless you change your ways you will not see the Light of Higher Consciousness. Now if you hear a voice telling you that, you will know it is the voice of the Higher Self.

Power Level IV

Sensory Impressions Through the Five Senses (Physical, Etheric, Astral and Mental)

This power is active on the sensory level, the lowest level of Power, and it is awakened by spiritual practices such as Kuṇḍalinī techniques, chanting, meditation and breathing exercises. When you do such spiritual practices you will begin to have what we call *sensory impressions* through the normal five senses of the physical body, as well as the subtle senses of the etheric-physical, astral and mental bodies. These include all kinds of sensory experiences, including seeing lights, colours, shapes and figures and hearing sounds.

Unfortunately, beginners on the Spiritual Path are much caught up in sensory experiences. They think that having such experiences is a sign of spiritual progress, that there's something wrong if they do not experience something in every meditation. In actuality, however, the sensory experiences you get when meditating, chanting or awakening Kuṇḍalinī are just that—sensory experiences. They are not an indication that you are making progress and have nothing to do with being spiritual. When you meditate, meditate; when you chant, chant. Forget about looking for sensory experiences. If you do that you will be wise.

True progress on the Spiritual Path is about one thing and one thing only: *Consciousness*. How far you have progressed on the Spiritual Path has to do with your consciousness, how much it has changed, not whether you have psychedelic visions or experiences.

The whole Universe is Pure Consciousness: transcendental, omnipotent, omnipresent, absolute, and without boundaries or limitations. In its original state your consciousness is also boundless, limitless and absolute, but your Soul-nature, mental nature, psychic nature and personality-nature are all limitations on your consciousness. The function of the Mystery School and spiritual practice is to get rid of those limitations so that you arrive at the stage of Pure Consciousness within you, where you feel yourself to be what you really are: boundless, absolute, eternal, beyond any conceivable limitation.

Sensory experiences are not the norm of meditation or spiritual work; they are just side effects. If you have them, fine; if you don't have them that's fine, too. What is important is *how much your consciousness has changed*, after each meditation, after each spiritual exercise; in other words, how far the consciousness rooted in MALKUTH (the Kingdom) has moved up the Tree of Life toward KETHER (the Crown), the Absolute Condition. So the aim of every spiritual practice is to free your consciousness so that it can move higher and higher up the Tree of Life.

PRACTICE

~

The Mantra of King Solomon

Now, let us meditate on the Mantra of King Solomon, who was a great, enlightened king of ancient Israel. The mantra is:

GIVE ME UNDERSTANDING AND WISDOM

This Mantra says: Let me ascend beyond my physical limitations, beyond my astral limitations, beyond my mental limitations, beyond the limitations of my Soul, beyond even the Great Divide that separates the Lower Creation and the Upper Creation, all the way to the Throne of God—Understanding (BINAH) and Wisdom (CHOCKMAH)—the omniscient, omnipotent, boundless state of Pure Consciousness.

Assume your favourite meditation posture and close your eyes. Say the mantra internally once, clearly and brightly, and then abide in silence. If your mind starts thinking, say the mantra again. Do this in your own time for twenty to thirty minutes or as long as you want.

The Mystery of Fire

Essentially, a Mystery School is a special school from many perspectives. You have to understand that it is not like a university or educational institution where you learn philosophical ideas and worldly knowledge. That has its place but it is not a Mystery School. And the function of the Mystery School is not to teach you about religious or spiritual ideas, however useful they may be. The Mystery School is way above and beyond that. The idea of the Mystery School is to change you *within*, until there is no division between you and the Divine: you and the Divine become one. What happens is that some part of supernatural *knowing* is implanted in your inner consciousness so that something is permanently changed inside you. You will no longer be the same because what will have changed is not your mind and its ideas but rather something inside you, on a profound level. So you have to understand and approach the Mystery School from this perspective.

One of the main themes of the ancient Mystery Schools was the Mystery of Fire, or the Journey of Fire. This *Fire* is the Spiritual Fire that takes you from "here" to "there", from mortality to immortality. The Mystery of Fire is a secret knowledge, a part of what the early Christians called GNOSIS and what the ancient Jews called CHOCKMAH, or Wisdom. Fire is the most mysterious reality in the Cosmos, far more mysterious than what the rational mind can imagine. So we are going to look at this most mysterious reality, starting with the first level of Fire, which is something you can identify with straight away.

1. *The Fire Produced by Rules, Regulations and Restrictions (Physical World)*

When you start working with Fire in a Mystery School, the first level of Fire is produced when you establish the rules, regulations and restrictions that are absolutely necessary for a spiritual school. If there are no rules and regulations there is no spiritual school. Full stop. You can't run a spiritual school if everybody does exactly what they like all the time. Not even a worldly organization can run like that. So a Mystery School must have rules, regulations and restrictions, which on the personality level cause annoyance, anger, inner turmoil and discomfort (the bigger the ego, the bigger the turmoil and discomfort).

To move towards a group enlightenment process, there have to be rules in order to produce cohesion, oneness and unity within the group, because if that doesn't exist the higher work is not possible. As an individual or as a group, you must be ready, that is, qualified, to move to the next level. For example, in ancient times groups like the Freemasons, Kabbalists, Rosicrucians and Alchemists talked about tests, trials and tribulations that one had to go through before they could be admitted into their groups. What I'm trying to say is that rules are necessary in order to transform a group to fit in with the requirements of the Mystery School.

So the first level of Fire is produced by regulations and restrictions, and you have to go through the annoyance and discomfort they cause so that you can pass to the next level of Spiritual Fire.

2. *The Fire Produced by Feelings and Emotions (Astral World)*

The next level of Fire is that produced by feelings and emotions, which means that it is connected to the Astral World. When the Spiritual Fire hits your emotional body you feel that your feelings have been hurt, so you experience activity in your solar plexus region, where your feelings, and your ego, are centred. This activity is the Fire working to purify your feelings, which causes suffering—which is the whole idea! But it's best to forget about your feelings and your ego and simply move on. Also, the Fire is doing you good because it is getting you ready for the next stage.

3. *The Fire of Esoteric Learning (Mental World)*

If you are a spiritual disciple, the Fire of the Mental World produces stress and tension inside you, caused by the new ideas of esoteric learning, which is not the normal knowledge you learn at school or in everyday life. Remember, these are not really *ideas* but *facts*; when you hear them, however, your mind treats them as ideas. They have to sink into your mind before you can realize that they are actually facts, and then they cause stress or tension because you have to change your way of thinking.

When new ideas are introduced to you, your mind (which is a closed energy-field) has a choice to accept them or reject them. This is why there are people in esoteric schools who always stay on the same level because their mind rejects them from day one. To accept them means you have to change, you have to open your mind to new possibilities, you have to go through the Fire of the Mind. Fire means burning, changing, and that is scary. Your mind is stressed out because you have to absorb all these new ideas, especially when you realize they are facts. You can take Spiritual Fire as a nice idea, but when you accept it as a fact it knocks your mind completely out of its normal way of functioning.

4. The Fire of Suffering: Hellfire

Hellfire, the Fire of Suffering, is also real. In the orthodox Christian, Jewish and Muslim religions and even in the Buddhist and Hindu religions, they talk about Hellfire as a place you go after death if you have been naughty. In reality, however, Hellfire is a liberating Fire that functions to burn out negative aspects inside you, either in the after-death condition or even in this lifetime.

Believe it or not, many people go through Hellfire during their lifetime because of sorrow or guilt, and it can be emotional, physical or mental suffering. They don't know that they're going through Hellfire. They keep thinking of the wrong they have done or that has been done to them, and they can't get rid of their sorrow or guilt. Something may have happened when they were a child and in their old age they are still going on about it. In order to liberate themselves they have to get rid of the guilt, sorrow or whatever is bothering them, *because it is no longer valid.* Their inner consciousness, their subconscious mind, is hanging on to it, which is why they are in Hell and will stay there until they realize that their problem no longer exists.

If they do not suffer in this lifetime they have to go through the suffering in the after-death condition. Then, when they go to the Astral World after death, they go to Hell there. They literally see a *fire* and it is trying to burn out that feeling of guilt or sorrow inside them. How long they stay in that condition after death depends on how deep their guilt or sorrow is and how much time it takes to burn it out and liberate them from those conditions.

Remember that when the religions say that Hellfire is eternal, they mean eternal in the sense of one's *experience,* not in the sense of reality. It doesn't mean that the Hellfire will be burning out your guilt or sorrow forever. What it means is that while you are in that condition in the Astral World, in the after-death condition, you have no sense of time. So if you experience Hellfire for one second, one minute, one hour, one year or ten years, it's always the same eternal continuum of experience. In that sense it *is* eternal, but only until you come out of it.

So it's important to assess the situation and look at what is here *now*. Is the problem really still here? No. If you hang on to it, you will just keep suffering. Hellfire is not necessary or compulsory but human beings are human beings and they undergo it until they let go of what they are hanging on to. The good thing about Hellfire, therefore, is that because you created the circumstances for Hellfire in the first place, you can dissolve them and stop suffering.

5. *Fire on the Spiritual Path: the Evolutionary Levels of Fire*

Now we are going to deal with the stages of Fire you have to go through if you are a serious disciple on the Spiritual Path.

(a) The Purifying Fire: Purgatory

The next stage of Fire, *The Purifying Fire,* is what the orthodox religions call *Purgatory.* The Purifying Fire occurs when you are actually walking on the Spiritual Path and, like Hellfire, you can experience the Purifying Fire while you are physically alive or in the after-death condition.

The teachings of the seven great orthodox religions say that after death there exist the Hell states, the Purgatory states and the Heaven states,[18] and that if you want to go to a heavenly state you have to go

18. Heaven, according to the orthodox religions, is the highest region in the after-death condition, which of course it isn't. The Heaven Worlds are certainly above the physical and astral dimensions, but the orthodox religions say that Heaven is the highest realm because they are not aware of the realms higher than the Heaven Worlds.

through the Fire of Purification, or Purgatory. This is totally correct if you are in the after-death condition: in order to reach the upper regions of the Inner Worlds you have to purify yourself first.

If you die with a low vibration, in other words, your personality is vibrating at a low frequency because you have been totally materialistic, in denial of yourself as a Soul and in denial of God and anything spiritual, there is obviously no way you can progress upward through the levels of the Inner Worlds. It is just not possible because the vibration of your consciousness in that condition is so dense that it keeps you in the lower levels of the Inner Worlds, which have a corresponding vibration. You definitely can't go to the Heaven Worlds! If you have not been too bad you will not go to Hell but to Purgatory, which is in the sixth dimension of the Astral World.

There, you go through the Purifying Fire, or the Fire of Transmutation. Since your vibration was heavy because your energies were materialistic when you died, you start having the sensation of a burning fire, which means that your particular personal vibration is being raised by the Sacred Fire and you are becoming lighter in vibration. You then feel yourself rising to a higher level of the Astral World and suddenly wake up to maybe the highest level of the Astral World. Then, as the Sacred Fire keeps burning you more and more, you begin to rise up through the Heaven Worlds.

But the same thing happens while you are in the physical body. You have to go through the Purifying Fire, the Fire of Purgatory, so that your *personality*-vibration is raised, just like in the after-death condition. Otherwise, you cannot approach the higher states of consciousness of the Inner Worlds because *by nature*, by the laws of Nature, there is nothing to move you there and everything to stop you from getting there.

So you enter a Spiritual School, you go to sessions, workshops and retreats and the Purgatory Fire begins to burn inside you, trying to make your personality-vibration high enough to receive higher-frequency vibrations. And this makes you out of tune and restless because you feel that you are neither here nor there: that you are in the world but not quite *in* the world, that you are in the Inner Worlds but not quite *in* the Inner Worlds. This is quite a traumatic process for everybody in this first stage of the Spiritual Path because what is happening is that your old self, your old personality, is being shaken up and purified.

By *purified*, we mean your personality is being lifted to a higher rate of vibration. The whole Spiritual School system is designed to lift your vibration: chanting will lift your vibration, meditation will lift your vibration, absorbing the energy emanated by the Teacher will lift your vibration. How well you absorb these energies determines how long your purification will take.

(b) The Fire of God Within the Soul

This is the next stage of the working of Fire on the Spiritual Path, and here you are on a high level of spiritual development. The previous stage of Fire involved the first stages of the Spiritual Path, where the Fire was burning your personality and trying to purify you by raising your vibration so that you could move upward into the Kingdom of God. But the Fire of God within your Soul occurs when you are already *in* the Kingdom of God.

All the great Sufi and Christian Saints and those who reached the state of Union with God talked about this Fire, saying that it was an intense burning fire within the Soul. This is way above the personality level; it is the Fire of God reorganizing your Soul, lifting its vibration so that you as the Soul can move onto another layer of Evolution.

You as the Living Soul live in the Causal World, where everything is perfect, every sensory experience you can have is beautiful and there is no stress about anything. It is just a perfect life. But at a certain point you will feel like you are under attack by the Fire of God, which will shake you up and urge you to move on to the other realities that lie beyond—the Buddhic World, the Nirvāṇic World and two other Light Worlds above that. You will reach this stage because it is part of the Mystery School system, part of the Spiritual Path.

(c) Cosmic Fire: the Everlasting Flame

The last stage is the Cosmic Fire. It is the last stage of the Spiritual Path and the last stage of the Mystery School system; it is the Everlasting Flame.

Cosmic Fire is the radiation that permeates the whole Cosmos, and the Everlasting Flame, which is the central part of that Fire, is the very essence of God Himself, the Divine Intelligence, the Divine Consciousness. So when you reach that level you have entered the innermost part of the Sanctuary and have become identified with the Inner Flame; you have reached the last stage of your Journey and are absorbed in the Everlasting Flame.

This means that you have become a Cosmic Being way beyond the human evolutionary level. You are Cosmic Intelligence itself, part of the *manifest* reality of the Divine Being—what the Christians call the HOLY SPIRIT, the Jews call SHEKINAH and the Hindus call ŚAKTI—the aspect of the Deity that expresses itself as the Reality of the Universe. You have identified yourself with the highest level of Fire.

PART IV

The Way of Transformation

Transformation of the Human Species

Supernatural Evolution

Evolution means that things change from one state to another, gradually improving in one quality or another. The scientific idea of evolution is limited to the observation of physical phenomena or physical happenings over the last few millions years, and as far as it goes it has more or less some truth in it. Things are always changing in the Physical World and you could call that natural evolution, or what Darwin called natural selection. Every form of life on this planet has evolved over a long period of time, so after millions of years of natural evolution the human species has reached its present stage of development.

During this vast period of time, your Soul has been incarnating over and over from the Causal World. There comes a time, however, when the Soul, having digested the vast gamut of experience it has accumulated, asks itself, "Is this all there is? What am I going to do for the rest of eternity?" Then you have a stirring deep inside you on the Soul level, what we call the *Great Awakening*. You are still in the natural state of evolution when that stirring starts, still the human being you were before, but suddenly something else comes in: you realize that there must be a deeper purpose to life or something bigger to attain or to become. This sets you on the track toward Supernatural Evolution.

Supernatural Evolution doesn't mean that you are going to have two noses and five legs, or that you have to become a bodybuilder with huge muscles. It is not about changing your bodily condition. Fundamentally, Supernatural Evolution means some profound changes occur *inside you*, on the level of the Soul. Naturally, because the Soul mechanism encloses your mental body, astral body, etheric-physical body and physical body, those bodies will also undergo change, but the biggest change is in your Soul itself.

Like Nature, Supernature also works by law. Science tries to discover the laws of Nature, and that is good, but it is not advanced enough to make laws about the changes within the Soul (or about the inner structure of the Universe). This is why the ancient Mystery Schools were set up by the Masters from the Spiritual Hierarchy: precisely to teach human beings what happens when they enter Supernatural Evolution. When Supernatural Evolution begins, a possibility opens for you to become more than what you are. Then you are usually guided to a Spiritual Teacher or Esoteric School where you find out what Supernatural Evolution is about and what you have to do about it.

In the Cosmos, nothing is given to you for free. On the Soul level you get a tremendous impulse for Supernatural Evolution, but from then on you have to actually start working out your Salvation. Remember, the Buddha said, "Work out your Salvation with diligence." The Christ said, "If you want to attain the Kingdom of God, take up your cross and follow me" (*Matthew* 16: 24). Nobody said that you can sit on your backside and watch TV all the time. Every real Teacher will tell you that you have to do something about your evolution. Yes, you will be inspired and you will have guidance, but you still have to work and you have to work very hard.

Symbology of the Supernatural Evolutionary Process

Now, the process of Supernatural Evolution is a three-part process, which is symbolically represented by the structure of the human family—Man, Woman and Child.

First, Man represents the Masculine Mind, the rational mind, the mind you normally think with and use every day. When you begin to work on Supernatural Evolution your rational mind must be totally surrendered, quiet and inactive. To do this, you need a lot of practice to make your mental faculty completely quiet and still, not criticizing, comparing and analysing, which are the normal activities of the mind. The average person is not in this mental state, but that is how it will be at the time the Great Awakening happens.

Next, Woman represents the Feminine Mind, which is the subconscious mind, also called the intuitive mind, the mind that *knows* by itself without the need to rationalize and think about things. Nowadays the Feminine Mind is totally suppressed and is not used by most people. Most people don't even know that they have a feminine mind because they are not taught to use it at school, at home or anywhere. The education system is based entirely on the Masculine Mind; everything is masculine and intellectual. But you have a feminine mind and that mind is in touch with the Astral World, *by nature.* This means that the Feminine Mind has sympathetic resonance with the higher realities, so it can know things that are not possible for the Masculine Mind to know.

Now, your Feminine Mind has to be completely open to the Supernatural Reality, open to receiving the tremendous impulses from the higher spiritual dimensions, open to the idea that you have to move onto a higher level of Evolution. So when your Masculine Mind is perfectly still and silent and at the same time your Feminine Mind is open and receiving the internal pulsations, the dynamic energies of the Higher Reality, then comes about the birth of the Child inside you. In Christian Mysticism it is called the birth of the Christ within you; in Buddhism it's the Buddha within you and in Hinduism it's the Kṛṣṇa within you—in other words, the Divine within you.

This is the stage of Supernatural Evolution when you feel that there is something else growing inside you, another entity that is not of your personality world. At first you do not notice it—you just have flashes of Supernatural Reality—but as the Child grows inside you, you become increasingly aware that there's the *you* that was you for aeons of time, but there is another *you* that is growing and evolving inside you. When Saint Paul experienced this he said, "I live, yet not I, but the Christ in me" (*Galatians* 2: 20). He was trying to explain that he was aware of being Paul, the human being who was doing all kinds of things in the world, and also aware that there was another entity inside him that was not of the world.

The Child will grow inside you, fed by supernatural forces and energies, provided that you keep doing your spiritual practices and live and act correctly. As you do your practices, your masculine mind becomes still and unobtrusive. At the same time your subconscious mind, the Feminine Mind, is open and beginning to sense the spiritual forces becoming active inside you. Year by year, as you continue to practise, the Child will keep growing until there comes a moment when you transfer all your being into the Child. You cease to be controlled by your two minds and you become the Child, the new being, the new You.

The Death of the Old and the Birth of the New

The new You can be born only when the old you has died. This is where many people on the Spiritual Path get stuck; they establish themselves in their old self, their normal personality structure, what they have been since childhood, and they want to stay like that, but at the same time they want to attain Enlightenment. They don't understand that that is not possible because Enlightenment requires change—a radical transformation, a *one thousand percent change.*

So the question is: Are you ready to die to the old? Everyone says they are ready to change, but change what? Their diet? Their job? Their partner? Their location? That's not real change. *You* have to have a fundamental revolution inside you and throw away the old self completely before the new self can be born. In other words, your Male Mind and Female Mind (your rational mind and subconscious mind) must have completely different attitudes before the Child can come into existence, let alone grow. There must be a fundamental change before the magical transformation can take place.

So what is this change? Is it about accumulating more name and fame for yourself or more goodies? No. *The change is in your consciousness.* You can be in a spiritual school or organization or practise Yoga for thirty years and be exactly the same as when you started. Yes, you will have a fit body and be calm and have a positive outlook on life, but fundamentally there is no difference because there is no change in your consciousness.

If you are like most people you actively resist change; you do not want to make even small changes in your physical life. So if you cannot change certain habits, attitudes and ways that you deal with things and other people on a basic level, how are you going to change enough to undergo the transformation needed for the Great Awakening? It's not possible. And that is why millions of people go on the Spiritual Path and do not attain Enlightenment.

It is important to understand that you cannot get there just like that. Without an Esoteric Teacher you can spend years and years and not get very far at all. If a five-year-old decides to climb Mount Everest, that would be a cute idea, but an adult knows that there is a lot more to it than just thinking you're going to climb the mountain. Yet people enter the Spiritual Path with the mentality of a five-year-old, thinking that they are going to become a great Saint or Adept, without the understanding and vision of where they have to go and what they have to do to get there. So you need the esoteric knowledge and meditation techniques that will take you there; you need a spiritual school based on knowledge, not theory, speculation, philosophy or theology; you need a Teacher who has direct knowledge of the Inner Worlds through experience.

Remember that you don't have to throw away your physical life in order to reach your spiritual goal. Buddha learned that the hard way. For twenty years he was on the extreme side of the Tree of Life, Severity, practising all kinds of fanatical techniques aimed at practically destroying the physical body, suppressing all feelings and paralysing the mind so that it would not generate thoughts. After twenty years of hardship, He realized that that was not the Way. The Middle Path is the Way, which means that you do spiritual practices without abandoning your natural state in the lower dimensions. You have relationships, you have a life in the world, and that keeps going on, even as you undergo this tremendous transformation I am talking about. You don't have to give up your responsibilities, you don't have to become a sadhu and do extreme things. Be as you are and maintain the proper relationship to all parts of Creation that you are supposed to as a human being, and at the same time work on undergoing this major transformation and rebirth: the birth of the new You.

In the Old Testament times this new being was called the new Adam. The Old Testament says that Eve came out of the rib of Adam. Remember that the Old Testament stories are only symbolic, but there is a real meaning behind them. Adam is the Masculine Mind and Eve is the Feminine Mind, and the Child, the new being, is both Adam and Eve. In other words, the Child is neither male nor female. It is beyond the distinctions of either the rational mind or the intuitive mind. It is a layer of Consciousness that is omniscient, omnipotent and omnipresent.

Supernatural Evolution does not happen all at once. Sometimes it can take a whole lifetime or even lifetimes; it is a gradual process and how quickly it comes about depends on how well you understand and intelligently cooperate with the process. This is why the teachings of an esoteric school are so important. The aspirants who go on the Quest but without any real esoteric understanding do whatever they think they should do. Then the whole process is very slow because they do the wrong things, things that ruin or obstruct the relationship of the two minds. So you need a proper Esoteric Teacher who will tell you what the inner work is about and how to do it, and who will help you to do it. Then your two minds will start working correctly and the higher energies will start becoming active inside you and produce the Child—the start of your Supernatural Evolution.

PRACTICE

Intoning the Mantra ELIYŌN, "God on High"

The Hebrew Mantra ELIYŌN is normally translated as the "Highest" or "God on High". More esoteric definitions of the word that the scholars do not know about are: the "Transcendental I AM", "Pure Consciousness" and "Pure Being". So ELIYŌN refers to God but not in the sense of the Creator God, the one who is active in Creation—that is ELOHĪM, the "Creator-Gods", the multiple Powers that are busy in Creation. ELIYŌN refers to the transcendental aspect of the Deity.

As a Living Soul in the Causal World, in the middle of the Tree of Life, you are caught in two directions. First, you are pouring your attention down towards the Lower Creation, towards the Mental World, the Astral World, the Etheric-Physical World and the Physical World. But a part of you, your Soul (which you are not aware of) is connected to the upper regions of Creation, the realms of Pure Consciousness and Pure Being, the realms of the Transcendental I AM. So when *you* (the "I Am" in your physical body) have gone through a spiritual rebirth and experienced yourself as a Living Soul, you can then make further progress and attain Pure Consciousness or Pure Being, the Transcendental I AM.

The point of this practice is to rise above your personal consciousness level and experience the part of the Tree of Life called GNOSIS, which means "Revelation" or "Enlightenment". In other words, you start with the sense of "I Am" in your physical body and then you reach the Soul level, where you have a sense of "I Am" as a Soul and you know your relationship to the Causal World, to the other Souls and life there. But you have to go beyond that and develop the sense of I

AM that is above all that, the indescribable condition that is the level of Gnosis. Then you will experience the real You, beyond the sensation of time and space; beyond the sensation of dualities (good and bad, hot and cold and all kinds of qualities); beyond thinking and every kind of multiplicity and all forms of energies. You exist as Pure Consciousness or Pure Being without any limitations or restrictions. This is the real esoteric significance of the Hebrew word ELIYŌN.

So intoning the Mantra ELIYŌN is about identifying with something higher than yourself. At the moment, as I said, your Soul identifies with all the lower aspects of the Tree of Life, your mental, emotional, vital and physical parts, so you can only make progress in the lower worlds, which, in itself, is fine. (For the materialists, it is perfect!) But if you want to reach beyond the natural state of the human being, you have to identify with something above that; you have to look upward. There is a beautiful psalm of King David—who was a highly advanced Adept—in which he talks about lifting up his eyes to the hilltops where God dwells.[19] So you have to re-identify yourself and lift your consciousness up *there*, where God dwells.

The practice is that as you intone ELIYŌN aloud,[20] try to lift your consciousness to a state above your personality level, above the limited sense of "I Am", to the limitlessness sense of the Transcendental I AM. Try to sense the I AM which is everywhere, which has no beginning or end, which just *is*. Try to feel the sensation of lifting yourself higher and higher up to a transcendental condition.

Now the next part of the practice is that you sit quietly in a comfortable position and intone Eliyōn silently, internally, focusing your

19. "I will lift up mine eyes unto the hills, from whence cometh my help. ..." (Pss. 121).
20. An audio file demonstrating the intonation of this mantra can be found at www.planetary-transformation.org/mantrarepetition.

attention as far above your head as you can. Imagine that you are looking upward at a great snowy mountain peak with the sunshine sparkling on it. Intone the mantra in this way, in your own time, holding the sensation that you are reaching up to the heights.

Baptism of Purification

The word *baptism* comes from the Greek word *baptismos*, which originally meant "initiation" or "purification". The Church used the Greek language in the early part of its history, and in the first 250 years of Christianity that word actually meant something for them. Nowadays, the real meaning of Baptism has been forgotten and it has become a religious ritual that you have to go through if you want to be a Christian. The esoteric significance behind the ritual has been lost.

So what does Baptism actually mean?

In the New Testament, John the Baptist said, "The one who will come after me will baptize you with fire and the Holy Spirit" (*Matthew* 3: 11 and *Luke* 3: 16). So besides Baptism by Water, there are two other kinds of Baptism: by Fire and by Air (or by the Holy Spirit or the Holy Breath).[21] So the real Baptism is a certain initiatory or purification process, according to a particular symbolism, that you have to go through before you can be reborn into the New Being. The Church may have forgotten, but in real life you still have to be baptized by Water, by Fire and by Air, which unfortunately the Church cannot do these days, not even the real Baptism by Water.

Water represents the Astral World, or the psychic dimension. *Fire* symbolizes the Mental World, the mind-structure. *Air*, *Spirit* or *Breath*

21. Baptism by Air is also referred to as Baptism by the Holy Spirit or the Holy Breath because to the ancients, in old languages such as Latin, Greek, Hebrew and Sanskrit, the words *air*, *spirit* and *breath* were the same word.

represents the Buddhic World, or Buddhic dimension. To put it in a modern context, you have to be purified first emotionally (the astral dimension/Water) and then mentally (the mental dimension/Fire) and then on the Soul level (the Buddhic dimension/Air). In other words, you have to go through a threefold Baptism of Purification or Initiation in order to purify the astral body of negative emotions, clear the mental body of wrong kinds of thinking and prepare the Soul for the Inward Journey.

Baptism by Water

Baptism by Water is necessary because the Astral World, which is like a gigantic ocean surrounding the planet, is normally polluted, just like the physical world but even more so. Your normal astral body is breathing in the polluted astral currents, which keep you bound to the particular degenerate conditions of the world. But within the astral dimension there still are pure currents of energy that are not polluted and *cannot* be polluted because they are kept as a pure source of Enlightenment energy working on the Astral World. These pure currents are called the Astral Waters of Purification, which, as far as the Astral World is concerned, are like pools of crystal clear water. Your astral body has to be "bathed" in those waters before you can start journeying up the Spiritual Path and be baptized by Fire and then by the Holy Breath.

The Waters of Purification symbolize certain spiritual practices (those used in a true Mystery School) that invoke the pure astral currents or energies to come slowly into your astral body and gradually free it of all negative energies so that it begins to breathe the beautiful astral radiances. When you sense a crystal clear radiance in your emotional nature, which feels like you have bathed in a refreshing, sparkling lake of clear water, you will know that you have received Baptism by Water.

This is what is meant when it says in the New Testament that John the Baptist baptized people "for the remission of their sins" (*Mark* 1: 4). The word *sin* was translated as the Greek word HAMARTIA, whose original meaning was "to miss the mark". It came from the ancient Warrior Schools, where it was a "sin" when an archer missed the target. So when John the Baptist baptized people "for the remission of their sins", it meant for all the things for which they "missed the mark", that is, all the wrong feelings, all the negative moods and emotions, all the negative desires in the astral body that had to be cleared.

Unless you purify your astral body, the Transformation process cannot take place. You can sit there for all eternity and believe in anything you want to, or not believe in anything, but if your astral body stays as it is, you will not make any progress on the Path. This is why people who have been meditating for years stay exactly the same, no matter how hard they work; they have not made the first step: the Baptism by Water, the purification of the astral body, the emotional nature. On a practical level, this means you have to start looking at your emotional patterns and letting go of all your negative emotions, dramas, past grievances—where you missed the mark, that is, you missed the true objective of your emotional nature.

Nowadays the way to deal with emotions is to endlessly talk about them, but that just locks you into negative astral currents and there is no way you can make any progress in this life. Your astral body must be restructured by energizing high-frequency vibrations. And that requires a twofold process: (1) by meditating, chanting and practising other spiritual techniques and processes that have a direct impact on your astral body and (2) by consciously working on your negative emotions. On a practical level, the spiritual techniques will help to purify your astral body but simultaneously you have to also consciously do something when you find yourself getting into a negative mood. Realize that negative emotions are not necessary at all; it's not compulsory to have them.

Once your astral body (that is, your entire sensitivity and emotional nature) becomes reasonably purified, you will pick up the higher, purer currents of the Astral World. Then you are ready for the Baptism by Fire.

Baptism by Fire and by Air

This is more severe than Baptism by Water, because your mind, or mental body, begins to burn and you become vividly aware of all your thought processes. A good example of this is Krishnamurti. He went through the Purification by Fire to such an extent that his consciousness was totally locked into his mental body and he was aware of every movement of thought in his mind all the time. This is an example of Baptism or Purification by Fire, but it doesn't have to be that severe.

After you have gone through some degree of Purification by Water and Purification by Fire, then you encounter the Holy Breath, or what we call the Purification by Air. Jesus said, "The air [Holy Spirit or Holy Breath] blows wherever it wishes and you don't know where it comes from and where it goes to" *(John* 3: 8). You experience the Purification by Air like a refreshing wind inside you, a wind that you cannot create or command because it is just a result of the previous Purification processes—but it is much more powerful and on a much deeper level than those processes, approaching the level of the Soul.

In other words, the Purification process starts with John the Baptist (Baptism by Water) and then moves on to the Christ (Baptism by Fire and Air). John the Baptist is like the human Guru or Teacher, the one who gives you the first motive force to start your Spiritual Journey; the one whom you first contact and who will tell you the way. Then you move on to the Christ, the internal Teacher, or if you like, the internal point of Divinity inside you. He will baptize you with Fire and the Holy Spirit. It's a gradual process and you have to go through it step by step.

In the old days these Purification processes were done on an individual basis. You had a direct relation with the Guru and he or she guided you through various practices and processes one on one. This has been the pattern for the last six thousand years, especially in the East, but it is no longer the pattern. What is different now is that Spiritual Schools like ours have an opportunity to work on a group level, not purification or transformation of the individual but of the whole School, the whole group—and *that* is a big difference.

This means that you, the individual, become important because all your actions impact on the group. If your astral body is not purified, your negative emotions will impact on your group, and it's your duty to change yourself. If your mind has not been purified and it is full of the wrong kind of thoughts, it's your duty to change yourself. In other words, what the individual does either hinders or helps the group process, so everybody has to be more responsible and go through their own Purification processes but in the spirit of helping the whole group.

You have to understand that a group process is miraculous. Just the idea of it is fantastic, and the actual practice of it is even more so. If everything works well, the group will move into the New Reality, a fantastic possibility of Group Consciousness in which everything the group does reverberates not only in the physical world but also in the inner dimensions. Then the group will pulsate with Light and the Light energies it generates will re-create the Astral, Mental and Causal Worlds. So as the group transforms itself, it transforms the planet, creating the New Reality for Humanity and the planet—the New Heaven and the New Earth.

The Secret of Death

All over the world, in every society and culture, people are afraid of death. This is because of the materialistic idea that when you die it is the end of your life, you're kaput, you cease to exist, forever. If you believe that, naturally, you are afraid of death because you want to live.

Then there is the religious idea of death. Religious people believe that there is an afterlife and the death of the physical body is insignificant because real life begins after that. What they believe is very true but the problem is, they don't really believe it. They believe it as a mental idea, not as a reality. That is why they treat the death of someone as a terrible tragedy. They believe that the person goes to a better world, the Heaven World, yet they still believe it is a tragedy; because in religion they *believe,* they don't *experience.* When you actually experience something it changes the whole picture.

For millions of years people have been afraid of death and they devised all kinds of rituals, customs and superstitious practices to cover up that fright. In society there is a fear of death because of the pure ignorance of what death is. In our School, however, we have an understanding of how things really are, so we know that death is not what society accepts it to be but a much bigger event, part of a natural cosmic process. To us, death is the Great Transformer; it is not the end of something but a transformation of something.

This Great Transformation occurs in the Cosmos all the time. Galaxies are born, galaxies die; solar systems are born, solar systems die;

planets are born, planets die; human beings are born, human beings die. So death is not the end of something but a transformation of something into something else. When you understand this, your ideas of life will change. You will be unafraid of death, unafraid of life, unafraid of anything because you understand the cycle of birth and death.

So what is this process of transformation?

> **Transformation is a change of form, a change of shape, a change of consciousness and a change of condition.**

Death simply means a change of form, shape, consciousness and condition. It's not a final ending or a disaster; it's a positive process. When something "dies", so-called, it becomes something else; it goes from one condition to another. It is as simple as that. When you understand that Death is the Great Transformer, he will become your best friend. As you walk with him through the Valley of Death, he gives you the Seed of Life. It can be quite a beautiful experience.

We are speaking about natural death, of course, and do not condone suicide or murder. Here is a quote from my book *Heavens and Hells of the Mind* about what happens to someone who commits suicide or is murdered.[22]

> The condition of the suicide and the violently murdered is very different from the case of a person who dies of old age or disease. The problem is that the natural life span of the physical body is cut short while the life-force is still manifesting outward and downward. ... [This] may be likened to a sudden tearing away of the body. There ensues a shock syndrome in one's consciousness and one is thrown into the hell worlds on the seventh level of the Astral Plane.

22. For more information about death, see: Imre Vallyon, *Heavens and Hells of the Mind*, vol. i, chap. 19 (Sounding-Light Publishing, 2007).

> Sudden death by violence or suicide embeds horrible and loathsome emotions and thoughtforms into the astral body of the victim, such as depression, fear, hate, anger, malice or an atavistic self-destruction complex. Since *you* do not change a bit when you cast off the body, these awful clouds of negative energies surround you on all sides and you live in a veritable hell. Suicides precipitate themselves onto the Astral through a distorted act of the mind, the penalty for which is terrible indeed.
>
> A distinction has to be made here between the murderer and the murdered. The murderer and the suicide can find themselves in the hell condition for a long time, but the *victim* of a violent act will stay in that condition only briefly—it could be a few moments or hours, or at most a few days—because that person has, in reality, no *affinity* with the hell worlds. The average man or woman has no affinity with those realms and will rise quickly to the appropriate astral region.

Rather than being afraid of death, therefore, you should welcome it because it is just a change. Unfortunately, people are afraid of change. They think every change in life is a big tragedy. They do not understand that change in itself is a positive value, that it is the very process of Nature and is going on all the time. Nature is always changing; *you cannot stop change.*

So you should never be afraid of change because all you are doing is changing into another form, shape or condition, but it's still the same *you.* In the Tarot, the skeleton is used as a symbol of death because skeleton bones last thousands of years. Scientist have found dinosaur bones that are millions of years old. To survive that long skeletons have to be pretty stable. So change is going on but the skeleton remains. You are changing but *you* always remain.

The Mystical Process of Death

Now we come to a deeper layer of Death, which we will explain. As far as human beings are concerned there are two major processes of Death.[23] One process is what the world is about and the other process is what true Spiritual Schools are about. In other words, there is the natural process of death that most everybody goes through and the Mystical Process of Death that certain people go through, which can include you.

We will give you a great secret—the Secret of Death—and we will start with the form of death that is most important: the Mystical Process of Death, which has to do with this truth:

The Fundamental Clear Light is seen when the ego is lost.

Here is the whole secret of the Spiritual Path. First of all, there is such a thing as what we call the Fundamental Clear Light, that is, the Original Light of the Universe, the Original Divine Radiance, the Ultimate Reality. In the Indian system it is called the Self or ĀTMAN; in Christianity it is called God and in Buddhism, Nirvāṇa. Whatever it is called, it is a brilliant white Light that stretches throughout Infinity, that has always existed and will always exist, and it is *fundamental* because it is the essence of Reality, the foundation of everything that ever happened or ever will happen in the whole Cosmic Reality.

Now, the Fundamental Clear Light is seen when the ego is lost, and there are two ways of losing your ego: at the moment of bodily death

23. As far as the Animal and Plant Kingdoms are concerned, there is only one natural process of death. This is another thing that distinguishes the Human Kingdom from the other kingdoms, including the Angelic Kingdoms. The process of death for the angels is not a sudden process like we experience but a modification of their being and their auric energy-field over a long period of time, without the idea that they cease to exist as in the human consciousness.

or in meditation. So you have a chance to unite yourself with the Light at the moment of your death or in your meditation processes while you are alive. (You also have a chance to perceive the Light at the moment of birth, when it appears to remind us of Reality. But it is difficult to grasp it at that moment because your physical cycle is beginning and it shuts out the Light. At the moment of birth and at the moment of death, however, the Divine Being gives everyone a chance to become what they really are.)

The chance to unite yourself with the Light is given to every single human being in this world. This is why Saint John said, "And this Light was in the world, but the darkness comprehended it not" *(John* 1: 5). Saint John was saying that the Fundamental Light is there for every human being but the human consciousness is in darkness and cannot comprehend the Light. In other words, you cannot perceive it because of your ego. The ego is that mechanism which enables you to function in the lower worlds (the Physical, Astral and Mental Worlds), but the ego is constructed in such a way that it blocks out the awareness of the Fundamental Light. As soon as the ego is removed the Light appears to you straight away because it has always been there. You do not have to create it; it's there and you just remove what is blocking it.

This is where meditation comes in. Through meditation and other spiritual training you gradually purify yourself until you have flashes of the Fundamental Light, which come more often until you can connect to the Light at will. Suppose you have seen flashes of Light through the meditation processes you have used during your life. At the moment of death when that Light appears it won't be strange or unknown to you. You will recognize it as the same Light that you experienced before and then you will merge into it. If you have trained yourself to see the Light through meditation during this lifetime but you cannot register it when the Light appears at the moment of death because of its brightness or for some other reason, you will recover the ability to register the Light slowly through the interdimensional processes because of your previous training. In the end you will evolve in the various Inner Worlds until you can register the Light and function as a Light Being.

So in both ways you gain, but either way, *you have to start the process in this lifetime.* You cannot decide to do it after death, because by then you have already missed the chance. Death is the Great Examination. The whole of life is simply a preparation for the moment of death and afterwards. If you have not done anything about it during your lifetime, you are lost. *You* are the master of your destiny, only you can prepare for your death; nobody else can do it for you.

At the moment of death you cannot change anything. Once you leave your physical body your destiny is one hundred percent set. You cannot change it, no matter whom you pray to. Whatever you do is what you will become. (Whatever you did is what you are now.) This is why life in the Mystery Schools, Tantra Schools and all the real Spiritual Schools was nothing but a preparation for death. In other words, real Spirituality—true Spiritual Teaching—*is* the Science of Death, what happens to you when you die. The true Esoteric Teachers tell you that you should meditate and live a spiritual life because the Great Examination will come and it will determine the next stage of your Journey.

Remember that the physical body only exists for seventy, eighty or ninety years or so, which in terms of eternity is meaningless. If you live a materialistic life and never think of anything except material things, when that bright Light appears at the moment of death, you won't register it. It will be like a big flash of lightning you have never seen before, so you won't know what it is and your consciousness will not pick it up. But if you have trained yourself in your lifetime to get in touch with the Fundamental Light, then when it appears at the moment of death, it will be like an old friend and you can embrace it.

So the Secret of Death is that at the moment of death you can attain the awareness of the Fundamental Clear Light. When you are leaving your physical body, the bright Light of Reality will appear for a second. If your attention is clear at that moment and you can embrace the Light, you will become liberated and will not have to go through the after-death processes in the Astral World and the Mental World. You dissolve into the Light and, technically, you leave the lower evolutionary cycles and worlds and you attain what is called Mokṣa, or Liberation or Freedom. You are a Buddha or a Christ, a divine being no longer obliged to function in the lower realms of Creation. You are free, forever.

The Natural Process of Death

If you miss your chance to connect with the Light at the moment of death, you move on to the next cycle, the natural process of death that the hundreds of millions of people go through. To understand the natural death process you have to understand two things: the sevenfold constitution of the Universe and the sevenfold constitution of the human being.

The human physical body and manmade scientific gadgets (no matter how sophisticated) are physical matter, material things, and they can explore only the vibrational frequencies of physical space and matter, and nothing more. But physical matter is only the surface of an infinite variation of vibrations or gradations of Matter. In other words, the Physical World is the lowest or the slowest vibration of the total Matter. Above the vibration of the Physical World there is another vibration of Matter occupying the same space but vibrating much faster. That is astral matter, the Astral World. And within the same space there is another even higher vibration of Matter—mental matter, the Mental World. In other words there is one Space with many gradations of vibration of Matter in different states and conditions.

In this room where I am talking, there are physical beings but there are also people in the Astral World and people in the Mental World. They are all in the same space, right here, right now; the only difference is that they have completely different vibrations, or energy frequencies, so they cannot perceive each other unless they develop a special ability. If people in the Astral want to see or experience physical beings, they have to densify their astral body vibration so that they can sense the physical vibration. Similarly, if the physical beings want to see the Astral World they have to increase their vibration so that they can register the finer astral vibration, and so on.

The lower worlds—the Physical, Astral and Mental Worlds—are just three of the Seven Great Planes of the Universe. These planes exist within each other in the same moment of time and each plane has a different vibration. Besides the three lower worlds, there are the Buddhic World and Nirvāṇa (the Nirvāṇic World) and there are two planes above Nirvāṇa. To experience those realms, you have to shift your consciousness to match the vibration of those planes.

The human being also has a sevenfold construction correlating to those planes but only up to the Nirvāṇic World; human beings have no possibilities above that unless they become superhuman and leave the human condition.

You have a physical body which corresponds to the Physical World and an etheric-physical body which corresponds to the etheric-physical part of the Physical World; you have an astral body (also called the emotional body) with which you can register and function in the Astral World; you have a mental body, or mind, so that you can function in the Mental World; you have a causal body with which you can function in the Causal World (the higher dimensions of the Mental World); and you have a body of Light that can function in the Buddhic World and one that can function in the Nirvāṇic World once you complete the Spiritual Path and enter the supernatural evolutionary stream.

The physical, etheric-physical, astral and mental bodies are what we call the personality or ego. As we said before, if you want to attain the Fundamental Clear Light you have to dissolve the ego, that is, dissolve the attachment to the ego. If you transcend the vibrations of your physical, etheric-physical, astral and mental bodies, then you go above the personality, above the sense of ego, and there the Light appears to you and you are enlightened.

That is what happens when you follow the Mystical Death as we described previously. But in the natural death process, when you leave your physical body, Nature takes over and you are embodied in your etheric-physical body (which is physical but invisible to the dense physical bodily senses). In other words, when you so-called *die*, you have not died; you have just moved into another form, condition and state of consciousness. You function for a while in your etheric-physical body—how long depends on how materialistic you were in your life. If you were very materialistic, you live in your etheric body but do not think that you are dead. You will go to see your relatives and friends who are still living and try to talk to them but they won't hear you. You feel completely like yourself because the etheric-physical world looks just like the physical world, just a bit more translucent, but you know that something is not quite right, not exactly how it should be. So you have to go through a period of adjustment.

After a while, Nature forces you to move on and you die in your etheric-physical body. This means that you begin to lose sensation of that body and start to sense your astral body. When you wake up in the Astral World, then again, you are confused because you can see and hear everything and everything appears normal to you, except that nobody responds to you. But the Astral World is definitely different—everything is more luminous and you can see through things—so after a while you pick up that you are in a different world and realize that you have moved on and are no longer a physical entity. Some people stay in the Astral World for a few years and some much longer, depending on their whole emotional nature and many other factors.

Then you die in your astral body and move into your mental body and are in the lower dimensions of the Mental World, which are called the Heaven Worlds or what the religions call Heaven. Now, to get into the Heaven Worlds you must have had some good karma. If you did not do any good in your life you would never get there because the vibration of the Heaven Worlds is based on harmony: the harmony of form, structure and consciousness. If you are not in a state of harmony, you cannot get to the Heaven Worlds.

Suppose you are in the Heaven Worlds because you accumulated a lot of good karma. There comes a moment when all that positive energy exhausts itself and you reach the end of your heavenly period. Then you face the Fundamental Light again—another examination, which we call the *internal* examination. (The other exam, when you died physically, was the external examination.) This is another chance for you to merge into the Light. If, like most people, you again miss your chance for the Light, Nature takes over and you start the downward process of reincarnation, which means the past personality is dissolved and a new personality is formed.

When you have gone through the whole cycle through the Inner Worlds and have completed your journey in the Heaven Worlds, the whole essence of your life is compressed into what we call the *Seed.* The Seed is an atomic structure, not a physical structure but a causal atomic structure, of what you have been. Scientists talk about DNA, which determines the characteristics of your physical body, so you could call the Seed your cosmic DNA; it holds the pattern of your entire past life up to the moment when you faced the final internal examination and failed. From that seed a new vibration is sent out and you start forming your first body, the mental body.

It will take some time until your mental body is fully formed in the Mental World. Then you go to the Astral World, where your astral body is formed, and then into the etheric-physical dimension, where your etheric body is formed. Finally you are born in the physical dimension; the cycle is completed and you start all over again.

The Seed shows that life is eternal. A seed is put into the ground, grows and then dies, but not before another seed is created. This is the natural process of death for ordinary people who fail the spiritual examinations. The whole cyclic process of birth and death is called SAMSĀRA, the Wheel of Life—you fail the exam, go into the Inner Worlds and come back. The whole process takes years and years of course; how long you stay in any world going up or coming down depends on many factors. Some people are so densely materialistic that they cannot register any fine vibration, so they are forced to come back into incarnation within a few years' time. Logicians, mathematicians, musicians, scientists or metaphysicians—people who have a high-frequency mental vibration—can stay in the Heaven Worlds for thousands of years. Regardless of how long it takes, however, Nature takes over and the Wheel of Life keeps turning.

But remember that the cycle of Samsāra is broken by Mystical Death—when you manage to dissolve your ego through the meditation process or by registering the Light at the moment of birth or death or at the internal examination at the end of your life in the Mental World. If you can merge into the Light at any of those times, then the Wheel of Life is broken and you enter Nirvāṇa. The word NIRVĀṆA in Sanskrit means "to blow out", like when you blow out a candle. So when Mystical Death occurs, you blow out the ego and in that moment you are one with Reality again. And this can happen in this lifetime or in the after-death condition or on the way back into incarnation—if you can recognize and grasp the right moment. This is the Secret of Death, the Great Transformer.

Your Options in the Inner Worlds

As you know, when you are born into this world your options and opportunities are based on many complex factors involving your family, your education, your karma, your own particular make-up, and so on. Your whole life here, what you can and cannot do, depends on these factors. Now in the Inner Worlds it is the same. When you die, therefore, you will have various options in the Inner Worlds, some of which we will try to outline.

When ordinary, nonspiritual people die, they have few options because they have to follow the Law of Nature. What they are going to experience after death depends on how they lived during their lifetime; in other words, it has to do with their frequency of vibration. If they have a dense, material vibration, like the vibration of many people during the Dark Ages in Europe, they will stay in the etheric dimensions for quite some time as what are called *earthbound spirits*. Their vibration, or consciousness, is so dense that they cannot sense any higher world, not even the astral dimension, so they can only stay in their etheric body, hanging between life and death, unable to follow the cycle of Life and either move on or be reincarnated in this world. They are the so-called ghosts or poltergeists that are associated with haunted houses and other psychic phenomena, which we will not go into here.

In the case of ordinary people whose vibration was not so dense, people who did some good things and some bad things in their life, they have a mixture of energies in them. They may have believed in God and had an idea about some sort of other-worldly life but put little energy towards that idea. So, depending on their emotional quality—in other words, whether it was a low emotional frequency, a higher emotional frequency or a refined emotional frequency—they will go to the lower, middle or higher dimensions of the Astral World. For example, people who were artistic and creative and used their emotions will most likely stay on the middle astral level because of their strong emotional energy. Those who had refined emotions, subtle feelings, will spend a lot of time in the higher dimensions of the Astral World.

As for the intellectual types, those who used their minds to explain everything and never related to their emotions, they will not spend any time in the Astral World because there is no affinity or energy to draw them there. They will give up their physical body and their etheric body and then go into what we call a sleep state, a lapsed condition or unconscious state, until they wake up in the Mental World, where their affinity lies.

So the average person will spend most of their after-death time in either the Astral World or the Mental World, according to the strength of their emotional or mental energy.

Then there are the people who started the Spiritual Path during their lifetimes. They may have followed a Yoga school or a Buddhist, Christian, Hindu, Sūfī or other religious teaching, or a Guru or Master. If at the moment of death they do not merge into the Primordial Light, then, like the others, they move onto the Astral World. At this stage, because they have started their spiritual life but haven't completed it, there are options available to them in the Inner Worlds, according to *how much* spiritual work they did, which is perfectly just. As with everything else, what a person does in their lifetime determines what happens to them after they die.

Now, if they did a lot of devotional chanting or had a high spiritual aspiration and their emotional body was strong, they will spend a lot of time on a higher part of the Astral World, what we call the lower heaven world. There they will go to devotional gatherings and listen to living Teachers and join chanting sessions or whatever activity is happening; in other words, they will continue their spiritual life on the Astral Plane. Here, two possibilities can happen: either they join a particular group in the Astral World, becoming the astral counterpart of that group and its living Teacher, or they become "freelancers" and enjoy the activities and then go and do their own thing. (Of course, this is what many people do here in this physical world: they go here and there and never really become part of any group.)

Naturally, if you were committed to a particular group during your life, you have the option of staying and working with that group in the Astral World. In our school, for example, we have between five and six thousand committed members, most of whom are on the Astral, Mental and Causal Worlds. On the Soul level they know that they belong to our group and are not interested in going anywhere else.

If you attach yourself to a particular Guru or group and follow their system and are faithful to their purpose, your karma (your destiny) will follow that particular energy-field from the Astral World into the Mental World. There, an interesting option is available to you. If you are attached to a true Teacher, you do not go into the normal Mental World as the other millions of human beings do, but into a specific energy-field that is generated by the group you belong to. You develop yourself in that energy-field and then at a certain point you are given an opportunity to work with the Primordial Light. If you manage to hold on to the Light at that time you will be liberated and technically you do not have to reincarnate; you can freely move about the Inner Worlds.

Now, if you are still not strong enough, or rather, if your Soul is not strong enough to hold onto the Light, then when your cycle is completed in the Mental Worlds, the Seed of your next life will be bright and strong because of all of the spiritual work you did beforehand. When you incarnate, therefore, you bring down a memory of working with the Light, which is translated into a high-frequency energy that you are born with and helps you regain the level of development you had before. This is why Yogīs such as Ramana Mahāṛṣi and Krishnamurti become enlightened at a young age. They recover some of the memory of their experiences in the inner dimensions or their previous life and are born with that seed in them already.

There are options for those who were, say, Roman Catholics or Buddhists or followed some religious tradition in their lifetime. When they are in the Astral World they realize that what they were taught was not correct or only partially correct. Then they have the option to seek a Teacher or school where they feel they can learn more. They can go to a Guru, who may or may not be in physical incarnation, and start participating in that Guru's inner spiritual school, even if they had never met that Teacher or group in their lifetime. For instance, we have an inner school and people in the Astral World can come and learn there. If they do, other options arise: they can start a life cycle with our group; they can develop in such a way that the Light will appear to them and they will have an opportunity to merge into it; or they can decide that they want to go along the Path of Service and choose to reincarnate because they realize that Humanity needs help.

Often groups of people incarnate as a team, not at the same time but over a period of one or two hundred years. During that time these Souls reincarnate and work as a team to stimulate Humanity for a particular purpose or in a particular way. Ours is a teaching group but it could be a group of scientists or a group of artists or a group of musicians born for the purpose of stimulating the planetary energy along their particular energy line. These people will then get in touch with Adepts and Masters in the astral dimensions or the mental dimensions who will give them deeper layers of knowledge so that when they come down again they become Esoteric Teachers. In other words, they are born into this world with knowledge that is not the normal kind of religious or philosophical knowledge: they are able to express the multidimensional nature of Reality.

So you have a number of options in the Inner Worlds to develop yourself and complete your Journey or, more importantly, to come back to this world and serve. The more highly developed you are, the more you realize that the world is full of suffering precisely because the materialistic mind is spiritually ignorant and destructive. The urging of your Soul directs you to come back and help Humanity become liberated so that our planet—now a planet of Darkness—can become a planet of Light.

PRACTICE

Contemplation

Contemplate the following statements and their explanation:

1. **The mind cannot go beyond the mind.**
2. **God is infinite and is beyond the grasp of the mind.**
3. **Find the source of the mind.**

The mind cannot go beyond the mind. This is the mistake of all the philosophers, all the theologians, all the scientists, all the mind-oriented people, because they are under the delusion that they can solve the ultimate meaning of life through the rational mind. There was even a group that called themselves the *Rationalists*—the most irrational people you can find! They denied that there can be any knowledge beyond the rational mind. But the mind is a structure—we call it the mental body—and because it is a structure it is limited, by nature. A limited organism cannot go beyond itself; a tree cannot be more than a tree, a dog cannot be more than a dog, and the mind cannot go beyond the mind.

You have your physical body, which is covered by your etheric-physical body, which is covered by your astral body, which is covered by your mental body, or your mind. So the mind is a large energy-field and within it are myriads of thoughts that constantly circulate. That's why your mind is busy all the time. But the problem is that people think the mind can solve all the problems of existence, can know the meaning of life, the ultimate truths and even God—which is of course one hundred percent delusion.

Statement two states: God is infinite and is beyond the grasp of the mind. How can a limited structure that only extends about two feet beyond the physical body grasp something that is infinite? If you think about it, you know that's completely impossible. So theologians or people who think that they can work out the nature of God or work out the infinite Cosmos and know all about it through their rational minds are suffering from a colossal delusion. The mind can only perceive according to its own ability of perception, but within that limitation it will try to understand and explain everything. And if something is beyond its grasp, it will refuse to believe that there is such a thing or will squeeze it into something that it knows.

I'll give you a worldly example. Many people have reported seeing UFOs in the sky, such as big globes of light or bright shining stars or multicoloured objects moving across the sky. But then the scientists come along and give their "rational" explanations. They say it was a Chinese lantern or a weather balloon floating across the sky. Or psychologists will say that the people had mental hallucinations or vivid imaginations. For materialistic thinkers, every phenomenon has to fit into *their* limited perception because they refuse to accept that there may be things beyond their possibility to explain. That is the limitation of the rational mind. The important point is that anything that has to do with infinitudes, like the Deity or your Soul-Nature, *cannot be grasped by your ordinary mind.* Forget it; don't even try.

Since the time of Atlantis, any experiences that people had which unveiled to them the grand mysteries of existence—the mysteries of the Soul, the mysteries of God, the mysteries of the purpose of life itself—were always experiences *above* the mind, never in the mind or with the mind. In the Tree of Life, the level of the rational mind is at the line between NETZACH (Victory) and HOD (Splendour), but when you experience Union with God, or see the Inner Space open up revealing the multidimensional nature of the Cosmos, your experiences do not come through the intellect but at the level of the Soul (TIPHARETH/Beauty), above the mind level. At the Soul level you can see into the heart of things, into the greater part of the Tree of Life, and you understand how Creation really is, how the Universe really is, what the real structure of the human being is—things that cannot possibly be known through ordinary logical thinking.

However, it's not enough to know that the mind is limited and cannot really know infinitudes or absolutes or higher realities. If your mind cannot explain anything real, the whole quest for the meaning of life is a waste of time, and there is nothing you can do about it. But there is a way: *Find the source of the mind.*

This is the job of the spiritual student. Keep the idea that the mind cannot go beyond the mind in the background of your meditations, as well as the idea that God, or the Absolute Reality, is infinite, boundless and timeless, and the mind cannot grasp it. There is a secret to accomplishing this, but if you find the source of the mind, you can move from that source back into the Infinite, or the Transcendental, that which is impossible to experience through the mind.

Glossary

The following are excerpts from *Heavens & Hells of the Mind,* Volume 4: *Lexicon of the Wisdom Language,* by the author.

Ādi

Sanskrit: The First, the Origin, the Source, the Beginning, the Primeval, the Primordial. Before all things, superior to all things. Also, "the First Plane", Mahāparanirvāṇa, the Logoic Plane, Satya-Loka (the Realm of Truth). Also, "the First Element", the Divine Essence, the Cosmic Element corresponding to the substance of the Mahāparanirvāṇic Plane.

Advaita, Ādvaita

Sanskrit: "Not two". Non-duality, Oneness, Unity. The All-Oneness.

Ākāśa

Sanskrit: Space. Heaven. The All-Light of Reality. Space in its totality as the physical body of God. "Space" does not mean some kind of emptiness in which particles of matter float. Ākāśa does not mean there is "nothing there"; on the contrary, Ākāśa means that *all* is there—total Fullness. To the ancients, the word *Heaven* (Space) did not mean just the physical sky, but the inner, invisible worlds and spaces as well.

Anāhata-Nāda

Sanskrit: "The Unproduced Sound", meaning "not produced by external means", heard in the Heart Centre.

Ānanda

Sanskrit: Bliss, Joy, Happiness, Ecstasy. The highest pleasure or enjoyment. Bliss is the very nature of Spirit (the Monad), and of You as a Soul.

ANIMA MUNDI

Latin: The Soul of Nature, the Soul within the World, the World Soul. The World Mother, the Feminine Divine Essence, Substance or Matter that pervades and animates all things. In Sanskrit, ALAYA-VIJÑĀNA.

Aquarian Age

As our Solar Logos (the Sun) moves about in space it comes under the influence of each sign of the Zodiac for approximately 2,150 years. Currently the Piscean Age is ending and the Aquarian radiations are beginning to be felt throughout our Solar System, changing, renewing, re-creating all things. This is why this New Age is often called the *Aquarian Age*. The ending of an Age and the beginning of a New Age is always *traumatic* for Humanity.

ARMAGEDDON

Hebrew: "Battlefield". From the Hebrew HARMEGIDDON (HAR, "mountain", and MEGIDDON, "the Valley of Megiddo"). In ancient Palestine there was a great battle fought in a mountain district called Megiddo, in Northern Palestine. In spiritual literature, the word ARMAGEDDON refers to the Battle between the personality and the Soul—the Spiritual Crisis.

ASCENSION

Latin: In the symbolism of the New Testament, *Ascension* is the Union of body, mind and Soul with God. It is the entry into NIRVĀṆA, the Kingdom of God.

ĀŚRAMA

Sanskrit: Stages of development in life. Also, a hermitage, a monastery or spiritual centre. In the West we call them the *Mystery Schools*. The Work of the Mystery Schools and ĀŚRAMAS is the expansion of Consciousness, alignment with one's own Higher Self, Spiritual Illumination, and service toward the Group Soul and the world, under the guidance of the Guru, the Hierophant, the Spiritual Master.

Astral Body

A form or vehicle made up of astral matter, existing on the Astral Plane. Every single entity—a human being, a bird, a tree, an animal—has an astral body. The astral body is a luminous form which interpenetrates the physical form. It is the more real part of your nature, for the physical form is only an extension of this luminous body. In Sanskrit it is called SŪKṢMA-ŚARĪRA (subtle body) and KĀMA-RŪPA (desire-body). Your astral body is your *dream-body*, in which you dream. In modern terminology it is known as your *subconscious mind*.

Astral Plane

"The starry realm". The sixth of the seven great Planes of Being. The Astral Plane is the world of the dead, where people go after they die. In the East it is known as KĀMA-LOKA, "the realm of desires". It is the realm of emotion and feelings, of psychic energies and forces, of the *subconscious mind*. The seven astral subplanes, or seven states of astral matter, correspond to the various heavens, hells and purgatories of the world religions.

ASTROLOGOS, ASTROLOGIA

Greek: "The science of the stars". The study of cosmic rays, energies and influences. The study of the motions of the planets in relationship to our Sun and how they affect Humanity collectively and individually. The science of the influence of the subtle radiations of the heavenly bodies (planets and stars) upon our Earth and upon Man. Hence the English word *astrology*. Astrology has been abused by the ignorant, the uninitiated, the superstitious. But the true science of astrology is a fact, and is just as real as chemistry or biology.

Astronomy

The science of the *material universe* beyond Earth's atmosphere.

Atlantis

Atlantean civilization extended over a vast area encompassing parts of the Atlantic Ocean, North America and Europe. Ancient legends and mythologies refer to that once-glorious civilization, but it was too long ago for people to remember accurately. What happened in Atlantis was not merely physical, but encompassed the astral dimensions as well.

ĀTMĀ, ĀTMA, ĀTMAN

Sanskrit: The Life-Breath of God the Absolute. The Self-Luminous Being, the Light of the Eternal, the Bright Eternal Self, the Spiritual Self, the Universal Spirit or Self within All. ĀTMAN is the Universal Divine I AM, of which Man is a part. It is the Innermost Spirit in Man, the true Man dwelling on the Nirvāṇic Plane, also known as PURUṢA (the Cosmic Man). ĀTMAN is the One Divine Self in the human species, the Universal Principle that gives the sensation of "Selfhood" to the Divine in Man.

AVATĀRA

Sanskrit: A Divine Incarnation. One who has descended from the Light Realms. From AVA (down) and TĀRA (to pass, to go), or AVA-TRĪ (to come down, to descend). There are Cosmic AVATĀRAS, Solar-Systemic AVATĀRAS, Planetary AVATĀRAS and Human AVATĀRAS—those who appear to Humanity and the Devas for the purpose of speeding up their evolution and aiding the Divinization of the planet. An AVATĀRA incarnates for a specific purpose. (The corrupted anglicized form is *Avatar*.)

BHAJAN

Sanskrit: Inner worship. Heart chant. Deeply devotional, meditative, contemplative, invocative singing and chanting.

BODHISATTVA

Sanskrit: "One whose very essence is Wisdom and Love". From BODHI (Love-Wisdom) and SATTVA (essence, being, quality). An enlightened Seer or Sage. A NIRMĀNAKĀYA whose essence is Love-Wisdom. An Enlightened Being who does not merge into Nirvāṇa but remains on the Buddhic and Causal Planes. A Buddha who sacrifices his or her own Enlightenment for the welfare of Mankind.

BUDDHA

Sanskrit: "Inwardly wide awake". One who is awake within himself. From BUDH, "to blossom, to bloom, to wake up, to know". This does not mean someone who is awake on the Physical Plane in the physical body. It means One who has awakened from the Sleep of Ignorance, who is awake on a very high plane of our Solar System, who is in a very high state of Consciousness.

Buddhic Plane

The fourth of the seven great Planes of Being. The Buddhic Plane has been called the *Realm of Unities* or the *Intuitional World*. It is a formless Light World characterized by Divine Unity, Love and Wisdom. The state of BUDDHI is Unitive Consciousness, Transcendental Consciousness or Pure Consciousness, wherein the Mystic experiences Oneness with the Universe and with God. The Sūfī Mystics called this realm 'ĀLAM-I-MALAKŪT, "the World of the Kingdom" (the Kingdom of God). In Christianity it is known as the *Christ Realm* or *Paradise*. In Sanskrit, MAHAH-LOKA. On this plane you are already Liberated.

CAKRA

Sanskrit: A circle, a wheel, a sphere, an orb, a revolving disk, a whirlpool of energy, a rotating centre, a wheel of fire. The term can refer to an atom, a planet, a solar system, a galaxy, a planetary vortex, or an Energy Centre in a human being. The Solar System is a large CAKRA, and each of the planets is a CAKRA within the Solar System. In a human being, the CAKRAS are subtle Energy Centres in the etheric, astral, mental and causal bodies.

Causal Body

The causal body (KĀRAṆA-ŚARĪRA in Sanskrit) is made up of matter of the three highest subplanes of the Mental Plane—the ARŪPA or formless levels. This is your Higher MANAS or Abstract Mind. Your causal body is the lowest part of your imperishable Individuality (ĀTMA-BUDDHI-MANAS), beyond your personality complex. Your Reincarnating Ego (JĪVA, you as a Human Soul) dwells in your causal body. Your karmas are stored up in your causal body, thus giving you the continuity of existence, life after life.

Causal World

The three higher subplanes of the Mental Plane, which are formless (ARŪPA). Also known as the *Archetypal World*. The Causal Worlds are realms of formless Ideas and Archetypes, which are the "cause" of all that manifests in the Three Worlds. (Note that the Causal Worlds are formless from *our* point of view.)

Channelling

From the Latin CANAL: "A waterway". Used nowadays to mean *mediumship*—receiving messages from the dead or from discarnate entities. Usually the medium speaks from her or his own subconscious mind. In rarer cases, an outside entity temporarily possesses the medium, psychic or sensitive and gives messages. Sometimes the term refers to the "channelling" of one's own Soul Wisdom, which has no relation to mediumship.

Christ

From the Latin KRISTUS, which came from the Greek CHRISTOS, which meant "the Anointed One, the Sacred One, the Holy One", one who has attained the grade of Supreme Hierophant of the Mysteries, after the custom in the Greek Mystery Schools of anointing an Initiate with precious oils and perfumes after he or she had passed all the tests and triumphed, or risen to Higher Consciousness. The Christ is threefold:

- Christ is the Great Being called MAITREYA, who is the Heart of our Spiritual Hierarchy (the Communion of the Saints of all religions).
- Christ is also the Spirit-Spark-Atom in your Heart which responds to the Call from the Christ of the Spiritual Hierarchy. Saint Paul called this "the Christ in you, your hope of Glory" *(Colossians 1:27)*.
- Christ is also the Splendour of God, the Cosmic Christ, the Cosmic Logos, the Original Word, through which and by which all things are made.

These three are one. This is the Mystery of the Christ.

Christ-Consciousness

Christ-Consciousness is Light-Consciousness. The Light of Christ, the Light of the World, dwells on the Buddhic Plane and descends onto the Astral Plane and hence into the Heart of the Mystic-Disciple. Christ-Consciousness is Intelligent Love, the human element combined with the Divine. This is the Mystery of the Christ.

CIDĀKĀŚA

Sanskrit: "The Self-Luminous Sky of Consciousness". The Infinite Space or Field of Universal Consciousness. The Boundless Ocean of Intelligence. The Wisdom- Mind which sees all things from above, from the point of view of the Transcendental Reality. CIDĀKĀŚA is ŚRĪ-JAGADAMBĀ, the Holy World Mother. From this Pure Consciousness come forth all things, and all things dwell in Her and are maintained by Her.

Clairvoyance

From the French: "The ability to see clearly". The full usage of the astral and etheric sight and, in its higher aspects, the faculty of Spiritual Sight. True clairvoyance is extremely rare. True clairvoyance is the opening of the Third-Eye Cakra, the ŚIVANETRA, the Eye of Śiva, the All-Seeing Eye, the Eye of Wisdom. The true clairvoyance of the Third-Eye is direct vision, as clear and unimpeded as physical vision. The Egyptians called the visionary faculties *The Eye of Horus*. Clairvoyance has seven levels, the last of them being the Absolute or Beatific Vision.

Cosmic Consciousness

The term *Cosmic Consciousness* can be understood in two ways:

- The condition of absorption into the exalted Consciousness of NIRVĀṆA, the Kingdom of God (ĀTMĀ-VIDYĀ).
- The integration of the Buddhic Consciousness (Pure Consciousness, TURĪYA) into the states below. In this exalted condition, therefore, the objective consciousness, the subjective mind (dream states) and the dreamless-sleep state have fused perfectly into the Transcendental State of Pure Consciousness. One is simultaneously aware of the four states of Consciousness, from BUDDHI downwards, while functioning in the waking state in the physical body. This state is known as TURĪYĀTĪTA-AVASTHĀ, "beyond the Fourth State".

Creation

The Universe is a periodic, or cyclic, manifestation. During each period of manifestation, God creates in seven great Cosmic Days, seven vast periods of Cosmic Time, seven great Ages. Notice, God *creates*, because natural and supernatural Evolution are still going on and will go on for myriads of years of Earth-time. Thus: Science has to understand what Evolution really is, and religion has to understand what Creation really is, for they are the *same*.

Creative Hierarchies

The human prototype is but one of twelve Creative Hierarchies of intelligent entities which inhabit appropriate planets, realms and planes of our Solar System. Each of these Hierarchies consists of countless entities. The Hierarchies are groups of lives, at various stages of unfoldment and growth, who use vehicles of expression (forms or vestures), the vehicles varying according to the spiritual development reached.

Crown Centre

The Energy Centre at the top of the head, also called the *Thousand-Petalled Lotus*. The Crown Centre is wholly spiritual. It will put you in touch with the spiritual dimensions and, ultimately, with Nirvāṇa.

Deva

Sanskrit: Shining, Splendid, Divine, Godly, Bright, Immortal, Radiating Light, Shining Substance. God or Divinity. Also, a Shining One, a Being of Light, a Resplendent Being, a Spiritual Being or Angel. Devas are non-human Spiritual Intelligences on another evolutionary line. They are called Malachīm (messengers) in the Jewish tradition, Angelos in Greek and Genii in Latin.

Devāchan

Tibetan: "The abode of the Shining Ones". The Shining Worlds. The *Seven Heavens*, the seven subplanes of the Mental Plane. The word sometimes refers to just the Causal Worlds, the three higher (formless) subplanes of the Mental Plane. In Sanskrit, Devasthāna.

Devatā

Sanskrit: The Shining Divinity, Fiery-Light, the Shining Fire-God, the Spiritual-Sun. Also, a god or goddess. Nonhuman evolutionary orders or hierarchies. The Angelic Kingdoms. Angelic species everywhere, as distinct from the humanoid species (Manuṣya).

Devil

Symbolically, the personality, which opposes the Spirit or Individuality. From the Greek Diabolos (an enemy, an accuser, a slanderer). It is true that there are evil spirits in the Universe, fallen angels and fallen human spirits in and around our planet. But no being is equal to God, so there cannot be an entity (called "the Devil") equal and opposite to God.

The "devils" (fallen spirits) came *after* the Fall. (Note that there is no such thing as the horned and hoofed monster, so popular with some Christians.)

DHARMA

Sanskrit: "That which upholds all things". The Force of Destiny. From the Sanskrit root DHRI, "to support, uphold, maintain, carry on, preserve, bear, nourish, foster". Truth, the Ultimate Reality, Justice, Law, Virtue. In the old Sanskrit understanding, DHARMA means the Path that you should follow to become what you are *meant* to be.

DHYĀNI-CHOHAN, DHYĀN-CHOHAN

Tibetan: "Meditative Lord". An Archangel or highly evolved Deva. The meditative gods. The feminine, receptive, group-conscious, selfless Angelic Hierarchies. Angelic Orders who are always conscious of the Eternal Unity, who have no separative tendencies, no ego, no self-centredness, no individualistic ambitions and plans. Their lives are always rooted in the Perpetual Light of Original Creation. (CHOHAN is a Tibetan word and the term DHYĀNI-CHOHAN is used mainly in Tibetan esoteric teachings.)

ĒGŌ

Latin: "I" or "I am" (EGO-SUM). The original meaning is the Absolute Spiritual Self or "I AM", the MONAD (Greek), the SPIRITUS (Latin), the Divinity in Man. Later on, it also came to mean the Soul, the ANIMĀ (Latin), which is within the body and beyond the mind. Nowadays, the English word *ego* refers to the personal self, the PERSONA (Latin: the mask), the personality or body-conscious "I", the unreal "I", the false sense of self (the Sanskrit AHAṀKĀRA, "I am the doer").

Elemental Kingdom

The Nature-Spirits of Earth, Water, Fire, Air, and the four etheric subplanes. The elementals are on the *involutionary* arc. They are below the Angelic Kingdom and below the Human Kingdom. The elementals are to the angels what the animals are to us: the Animal Kingdom is one step below the Human Kingdom in evolutionary attainment, and the Elemental Kingdom is one step below the Angelic Kingdom. The normal habitat of the elementals is the Astral World. Some elementals have an etheric body, but they never have a gross physical body. Sometimes they can be seen in their etheric bodies, and folklore has called them by many names according to their species: dryads, naiads, oreads, kelpies, leprechauns, fairies, nature-spirits, brownies, mannikins, fauns, satyrs, centaurs, and so on.

ELOHĪM

Hebrew: "The Self-Born Gods" (male/female plural). The KOSMOKRATORES (Greek). The Cosmic Creator-Gods, the Spirits who manifest suns, planets and Cosmic Systems of Evolution. The Solar Logoi. Our own Solar Logos, the Sun, is known in Sanskrit as BRAHMĀ, ĪŚVARA or SAVITĀ. The Creator-Gods are not the Angelic Hierarchies, but are far above them. The angels came into being *after* the Creator-Gods had already fashioned the Universe. In *Genesis*, first appear the ELOHĪM, the male-female Creator-Gods, but the patriarchs did not like this fact because they wanted the work of all Creation to be done by only one Person. In later chapters it becomes ELOHĪM-JEHOVAH; then, by the time of Moses, it became JEHOVAH. The church fathers, and before them the Jewish patriarchs, wanted to *deny* the existence of these great Beings—the ELOHĪM, the KOSMOKRATORES, the Creators of the Cosmos. But they need not have done so, for there is only one Absolute Reality, one Godhead under which all Beings work—great or small, cosmic or atomic.

Etheric Body

The etheric body exists on the etheric subplanes and is made up of the four states of etheric-physical matter. It is the vehicle of PRĀṆA, vitality, the Life-breath. It is also known as the *etheric-physical body*, the *subtle-physical body*, the *vital body* or the *etheric double*. In Sanskrit it is called LIṄGA-ŚARĪRA (symbolic body) because it is the prototype and Life-force of your dense physical body.

Etheric Web

An energy-structure within the etheric body which protects a physically embodied being from an influx of energies from the Inner Worlds. A human being has an etheric web, as does a planet and a solar system. At an advanced stage of human evolution the etheric web is burned away by the Kuṇḍalinī Fire, thus leading to Continuity of Consciousness and Cosmic Consciousness.

Evil

Evil means "physical imperfections and mind-created hell worlds". Evil is the wrong use of the One Force, Power, Energy or Substance (ŚAKTI) by living entities, whether through Ignorance or lack of Intelligence. Evil is caused by separative minds that do not feel and do not know the Unity of all Life. These evil minds can be human, subhuman (elemental) or angelic.

EVOLUTION

Latin: Unfolding, progression, metamorphosis, formation, growth, development, mutation, an unrolling, an opening up, a process of gradual, progressive change. There is a natural evolution (*horizontal* evolution) and there is a supernatural, spiritual evolution (*vertical* evolution). The scientific theory of natural evolution is correct but science hasn't even thought about the Supernatural Evolution.

Fall

The idea of "the Fall" can be understood on two levels:

- The descent of the Human Monads (Virgin Spirits) from the formless Causal Worlds into the material conditions of the Three Worlds, henceforth losing Awareness of the Immortal Luminous Oneness while cycling endlessly through the material realms (SAṀSĀRA). The Old Testament story of Adam and Eve being tempted by the serpent is symbolic of this event (the serpent being the KUṆḌALINĪ-ŚAKTI, the Evolutionary Force).
- The separation of a vast host of originally-luminous angels from the Primary State of Unity, millions of years ago, thus corrupting certain parts of the Omni-Revelation of the All-Mind. We cannot know whether the "fall" of these angels was by Cosmic Design or an act of free will. When the human family descended onto this planet it became caught up in the Cosmic Evil and has perpetuated it ever since.

Father

In Christianity, a symbol for the First Aspect of the Holy Trinity, the Eternal Cosmic Being, the First Logos. On a human level, the term "Father" or "Father in Heaven" symbolizes the MONAD, the Divine Spirit in Man (PARAMĀTMAN, the Transcendental Self, dwelling on the Paranirvāṇic Plane). In the New Testament the Eternal Cosmic Being is called "Father" due to the sexual bias of the old Jewish religious concepts.

GANDHARVA

Sanskrit: Music-Angel. This Sanskrit word is most esoteric. It refers to the Sound-Angels, the Celestial Angelic Musicians, the nonhuman (angelic) Intelligences which produce the sounds and colours in the Inner Worlds. The GANDHARVAs live by creating the most exquisite music, sound, tone, colour and harmony in the Astral World. They like events which include music, singing or dancing and often add their musical skills on the Astral to produce glorious effects.

GĀYATRĪ-MANTRA

Sanskrit: The most sacred Mantram of India. Also known as the SAVITĀ-Mantra, the SŪRYA-Mantra, the SAVITṚ-Mantra or ŚIVA-SŪRYA. This Mantra invokes the Male Aspect of the Solar Logos (the Solar Logos is Male-Female-Neuter, all at once). This is the Mantra for Enlightenment, Illumination, Transfiguration in Light, moving with the forces of evolution, progress, development. The GĀYATRĪ is a prayer, not a relaxation technique; it should never be repeated after a Haṭha Yoga class as a relaxation exercise.

God-Consciousness

The term *God-Consciousness* (BRAHMĀ-VIDYĀ) can refer to the following conditions:

- The State of Union with the Divine Being, the Monad, the "Father in Heaven" (PARAMĀTMAN). Also called *Divine-Consciousness*.
- The integration and fusing of the Nirvāṇic Consciousness (ĀTMĀ-VIDYĀ) into the states below.

GURU

Sanskrit: The Illuminator, the Dispeller of Darkness, the Bringer of Light, the Enlightener. The Transcendental Wisdom of God (BRAHMAN), of the Self (ĀTMAN), and of your physical Teacher or Preceptor. Sometimes called GURUDEVA (Divine Teacher) or SAT GURU (True Master). The Master or Spiritual Guide—the Guide of your Soul, not of your personality! Nowadays the word *guru* is commonly used to refer to a mentor or advisor, or any person who gives religious instructions, or an intellectual guide, or any leader or authority in any field. The original Sanskrit word GURU has only a deeply *religious-spiritual* meaning.

HAMARTIA

Greek: "Missing the mark" (as in archery). This is the Greek word the scholars and theologians so morbidly translate as "sin", in the sense of devaluing yourself and destroying your self-esteem. The word *sinner* has acquired, in Christianity, a very unhealthy connotation. But the Greek word actually means "to miss the mark, to miss the point, to go astray, to make a mistake, to falter or fail, to make an error". There is no sense of "eternal hell-fire and damnation" in it, as proclaimed by the evangelicals and fundamentalists of today's Christianity. The correct meaning is that you *try again*. If you failed in some aspect of your nature, you do not thereby become morbid, depressed and negative, but you try again and again. This is how the early Christians looked upon life.

HAṬHA YOGA

Sanskrit: The best-known branch of Yoga in the West, HAṬHA Yoga consists of ĀSANAS (postures), PRĀṆĀYĀMAS (breath-controls), MUDRĀS (seals), BANDHAS (restraints) and ŚAT-KRIYĀS (purificatory exercises). It is sometimes called the "physical" Yoga, or the Yoga of the body, because it emphasizes the subjugation of the physical vehicle and the balancing of the "Sun" and "Moon" currents in the etheric body. Nowadays, Haṭha Yoga is thought to be nothing but keep-fit exercises. By the ancient definition, however, Haṭha Yoga has nothing at all to do with "keeping fit". Haṭha Yoga focuses on the *subjugation* of the physical body.

Heart

The Heart is *not* the heart in your physical body. It is a *psychic-spiritual* Heart located near the physical heart, in the subtler dimensions. There are three regions of the Heart:

- The *physical heart*, located in the physical body in this three-dimensional world.
- The *psychic Heart*, connected to your psychic being on the fourth-dimensional level of Space (the astral body).
- The *Spiritual Heart*, the centre of your true Self or Spirit, on the sixth-dimensional level of Space (Buddhi) and above.

The Mystics of Judaism, Christianity, Islam and Hinduism concentrate in the Heart to discover the Path that leads to "the Kingdom of God within"—the Higher Consciousness.

Heaven

In the language of the Old and New Testaments there is a shortage of words to describe Spiritual Realities. For instance, the word *Heaven* (or *Heavens*) is used to signify the sky, the starry space above, the after-death worlds, the Kingdom of God, and so on. *Heaven* is called SHEMAYĀ in Aramaic, SHAMAYĪM in Hebrew, OURANOS in Greek, CAELUM in Latin. In each of these Western languages which relate to original Christianity, *Heaven* means the multi-dimensionality of Space, as a Unity or Oneness, as a Continuum between the within (the above) and the without (the below).

Heaven Worlds

The *lower heavens* are the higher, subtler regions of the Astral World. These regions of the Astral World are more rarefied, artistic, intellectual, scientific, creative and religious than the regions below. People in this realm mistakenly call it "Heaven". The true *Heaven Worlds*, however, are the seven subplanes of the Mental Plane, known in the East as DEVA-STHĀNA, "the abode of the gods" (DEVĀCHAN in Tibetan), and in the Christian religion as the *Seven Heavens*.

Hell Worlds

The seventh subplane of the Astral Plane of this Earth-planet. This realm lies in the fourth dimension, partly on the surface of the physical Earth and partly below it, in the solid crust. The experience of "Hell", as described by thousands of people and by all world religions, is real. "Hell" is quite literally a product of the sufferer's mind, as is the "Heaven" of a more saintly person, because *mind* (whether human or angelic) creates the outer environment in which an entity lives.

Holy Spirit (Holy Ghost)

The Holy Breath, Holy Life-Force, Holy Intelligence, Holy Creative Power. The Radiant Creative Energy, the Fire of Creation. The Cosmic Fiery Energy of the Third Logos, the Third Person of the Trinity. The Holy Spirit is the Immanent Deity (BRAHMĀ, in Sanskrit), that which is concealed in matter, life-forms, bodies. It is God-in-Manifestation, the Embodied God. It is the Organizing and Structurizing Power within the Universe, God's Divine Mind at work, or Cosmic Intelligence. Also known as SHEKINAH (the Divine Presence) in Hebrew, and ŚAKTI (the Divine Energy) in Sanskrit.

ĪŚVARA

Sanskrit: "The Lord-God". The Master, Ruler, Controller, Director. The Supreme Being, the Cosmic Spirit, the Central Intelligence of the Universe, the Highest Authority in the Cosmos. The Lord of All, the Lord of the Universe, the Chief among All, the King of Kings, the Lord of Lords, the Master Power, the Inner-Ruler-Immortal. ĪŚVARA is the Heart Centre, or Centre of Consciousness, in any system, microcosmic or macrocosmic. It is the power of Lordship and independent action, the ruling, guiding or controlling principle within.

Jesus

The word *Jesus* comes from the Latin IESUS and IESU, which were derived from the older Greek IESOUS and the still older Hebrew and Aramaic YESHUA, YOSHUA, YEHESHUA, YEHOSHUA or YEHESHUVAH. As a Jewish child He probably would have been known as YOSHUA (JOSHUA). Like the peoples of India, the Jews gave Divine Names to their children. YEHESHUA means "the Eternal is my Salvation, in God is Salvation, God is my helper". YESHUA means "Saviour, Deliverer, Salvation, the Power to Save or Liberate, God's downpouring Grace". Hence, *Jesus* means "the Saviour".

Jesus Christ

A compound of Hebrew and Greek words meaning "a Divine Teacher or Guru who has been anointed, or who has been acknowledged as succeeding in the Mysteries of Life and Death". The name "Jesus Christ" is correctly *Jesus the Christed One* (in the original Hebrew, YEHESHUAH HA-MASHIAH).

KALI YUGA

Sanskrit: "The Dark Age" (this is not a reference to the Dark Ages of European history). KALI YUGA is the Age of materialism, ignorance and darkness. We live in the Age of KALI YUGA. In this Age materialism prevails, spiritual ignorance and blindness, called MĀYĀ. The peoples of the Earth are blinded by material energies, material powers, material objects. The lives of people are taken up with accumulating material objects for themselves and their families. Material comforts supersede spiritual powers. Name and fame in society supersede the true Kingliness and Majesty of the Perfected Man.

Karma

Sanskrit: "Action". Cause and effect, action and reaction, the effect or results of action. From the root Krī, "to do, to act, to perform". Karma is the Law of Cause and Effect, the Universal Law governing all actions: past actions causing present events, and present actions causing future events. Every action has a corresponding reaction; that is, the reaction is *in kind.* In the Jewish, Christian and Muslim religions, karmas are called "sins"—transgressions against the Laws of Nature, which are the Laws of Mind. All actions are caused by some mind; therefore, Karma rules Mind. The Lord Buddha called it "the Good Law".

Kingdom of God

The expression *The Kingdom of God* can represent several things:

- The invisible Spiritual Hierarchy.
- Specifically, the Nirvāṇic Plane.
- Generally, all the invisible planes.

The flow of the great Revelation of the Kingdom of God presses downward from Nirvāṇa throughout the ages: down through the Buddhic Plane, the Causal Worlds, the Mental Plane and the Astral Plane, finally manifesting on the Physical Plane, in this Physical World.

Kīrtana

Sanskrit: Devotional singing and dancing. Devotional chanting, which stirs the Śabda, the God-Incarnating Sound. Also, Sankīrtana.

Lemuria

The third great epoch, or Root-Race, of human evolution upon this planet, preceding Atlantis. The Lemurian epoch concerned itself with the Physical Plane, with the evolution of the gross physical body and the two lowest cakras—the Base Cakra and the Sex Cakra. The physical body of Man has since been slowly evolving over countless millennia. The Lemurian epoch led to gross magic, black magic, earth-control, and so forth. During this epoch, people could not "feel".

Liberation

The Freedom of the Soul from birth and death in the lower worlds (Saṁsāra, wandering). Freeing your consciousness from the pains, delusions and errors of the lower worlds and experiencing the realms of Buddhi and Nirvāṇa. Being able to live freely in the Spirit, unhindered by your physical body, mind and personality structure. Conscious

Immortality. In the West this is known as *Salvation* and *Beatitude*. In Sanskrit, MOKṢA (Freedom) and MUKTI (Liberation).

Light

Light is not a metaphor or a symbol. It is real. In fact, it is the only Reality! Light is God-in-Manifestation, God-in-Incarnation, God-in-Expression. Light is God's Presence in Creation. Light is living, conscious, substantial Intelligence. Your Soul is made out of It. The physical light of the Sun, Moon and stars is but a fragment of Light. Light is Substance, Matter of a higher order, many invisible grades of Substance and Essence. Light is many-layered, multidimensional. The Light may be found in the Heart Centre, in the Third-Eye Centre and in the Crown Centre. Light is a Field of Energy emanated by God. When you see the Inner Light, you are *close* to God.

Limbo

The *limbo* states are states in the etheric-physical body on the subtle levels of the Physical Plane. This is the realm of the "ghosts", the earthbound spirits. Sometimes this term refers to the purgatory conditions of the Astral World.

Living Soul

Sanskrit: The Human Soul, dwelling on the formless subplanes of the Mental Plane and reflecting the triune nature of the Universal Being as ĀTMA-BUDDHI-MANAS. The Living Soul is below the Spiritual Soul (BUDDHI), which is in turn below the Spiritual Self (ĀTMAN). Called JĪVA or JĪVĀTMAN in Sanskrit, PSYCHE in Greek, NAFS in Arabic. In the East it is called the *Thinker* and the *Reincarnating Ego* because it takes on a new personality with each new incarnation. When functioning through the personality it is known as AHAṀKĀRA, "I am the doer". This is the personality's sense of "I am".

LOGOS

Greek: To the Greek Mystery Schools, the LOGOS was the Creative Word of God, the Universal Creative Intelligence, the Wisdom of God as a *Power*, the Source of Creation, the Cosmic Fatherhood, the Source of all things, the Creative God who created the Universe and in whom the Universe exists (Cosmic Logos), or who created the Solar System (Solar Logos). The Christians borrowed this idea from the Greeks: the LOGOS is the "Word" of the Christian Bible. The Christian fathers adapted the LOGOS doctrine to Christianity as follows: the *Father* is the First Logos; the *Son* (or Christ) is the Second Logos; and the *Holy Spirit* is the Third Logos. Yet there is only One God (One Cosmic LOGOS).

Love

Love is an Energy. It is not just a thought or a nice idea. It is a Force, a Power.

- There is personality Love.
- There is Soul Love (Group Love).
- There is Divine Love (Cosmic Love).

Love is not sex. The sexual energy is astral-etheric. In a human being the Energy of Love is found in the Heart Centre.

Lower Mind

The rational mind or concrete mind. In Sanskrit, RŪPA-MANAS (form-mind). It is the activity of the mental body (MĀNASA-RŪPA), functioning on the lower (form) levels of the Mental Plane. This is the common mind, the ordinary intellect, which is connected to the region of the brain between the physical eyes. Most people nowadays are stuck in the brain-mind due to the influence of their upbringing and the worldly education system.

MAITREYA

Sanskrit: "The Compassionate One". Friendly, compassionate, benevolent. It was the Lord Christ, ĪŚA-MAITREYA, who overshadowed that Great Master who was called JOSHUA (Jesus). MAITREYA is the World Teacher, the Teacher of Angels and Man, who is responsible for the spiritual development of the Angelic species and Mankind upon this planet. MAITREYA looks after all religious development upon this planet through His agents, the Spiritual Teachers, Saints, Yogīs, Adepts and Mystics, in all religions (Christianity being but one of them). MAITREYA is the Heart of the Spiritual Hierarchy of our planet.

Man

Man is an old English (Teutonic) word, synonymous with the Latin HOMO and the Hebrew ADAM, which means "a human being, a human creature", as distinct from the Animal, Vegetable or Angelic Kingdoms. The word *Man* refers to the human species, the genus of the human race, of both male and female genders. It does not mean only males. *Man* or *Mankind* is "the two-legged species with the thinking brain." Esoterically, *Man* is that Being in the Universe in which the highest Spirit (the Monad) is conjoined to the lowest matter (the physical body) by the Intelligent Principle (the mind). In Sanskrit, MANUṢYA or NARA.

MANAS

Sanskrit: Mind. The ruling, regulating, creative, ordering principle. The intelligent purpose of some being, working out into active objectivity. In Man, the principle of MANAS has two aspects:

- Higher Mind, KĀRAṆA-MANAS (Causal Mind), which is abstract and formless.
- Lower mind, RŪPA-MANAS (form-mind). The lower mind is usually tinged with desire, thus producing KĀMA-MANAS (desire-mind).

MANTRA, MANTRAM

Sanskrit: "An instrument of the mind, a thinking-tool, an instrument of thought, a mental creation, a thought-vibration". From MANAS (mind) and TRA (a tool or instrument). TRA also means "to transcend" and "to protect". Thus, a Mantra is an instrument of your mind, it protects your mind, and it also helps you to transcend the mind. Mantra is most often identified with *sound.*

A Mantra is a sound-formula outwardly chanted, intoned or sung, or inwardly spoken, sung and *realized.* Mantras, in Sanskrit, Hebrew, Arabic, Greek, Latin and Chinese, are energy-units to stimulate your Higher Evolution and your Transformation into the likeness of the God-Being within you.

MANVANTARA

Sanskrit: "Day of God". A Day of Creation, a Day of Manifestation, a Creation or Cycle of Evolution. The period or age of the creation and continuation of an object in Space. A period of Evolution, large or small. At the end of Creation, when the Evolutionary processes are completed, all is reabsorbed into PRALAYA, which is absolute Rest, the pre-cosmic Divine Darkness, the Night of God.

Materialism

The belief in objective matter existing on its own, without the Being of God. The false view that physical matter is all that constitutes the Universe, that mind, Soul and Spirit are but material activities (the brain, nervous system, etc.). Materialists do not have open minds. Their minds are blocked by the false assumption that what they can sense with their physical senses is all that exists. Both orthodox religion and orthodox science are produced by the personality and serve the false, limited sense of ego or "I", the personality sense. They are the limited personality's view of Reality, not Reality as it really is, beyond the five senses.

MEDITATION

Latin: Originally, the Latin word MEDITATION meant "to contemplate Reality, to focus on Reality". This original meaning is radically different from the current usage of the word; only in later times has it come to mean "to think, to reflect, to ponder over a problem". Meditation is a search for Reality. Because Reality is not understood, however, meditation is not understood. This New Age of Aquarius is an extremely materialistic age; therefore, even meditation has been twisted into a quest for material progress. As defined in Mysticism, meditation is "a quiescent, prolonged, spiritual introspection; a devout religious exercise". Meditation is a quest for the Real, the Imperishable, the Eternal One.

Mediumship

Contacting the dead or one's "spirit-guides", the so-called "angelic beings", "masters" or "space brothers". Ordinary mediums (nowadays called "channellers") receive their messages from their own subconscious minds, or by allowing a spook on the Astral Plane to speak through them or use their etheric voice-box mechanism, which requires that energy (ectoplasma) be drawn from the etheric body of the medium and those in the seance or circle. Mediumship destroys your Soul's evolution because it locks your consciousness into the Astral World.

Mental Body

The vehicle of the lower mind, the concrete mind, the lower MANAS, existing on the lower four subplanes of the Mental Plane (those with form). In Sanskrit, MĀNASA-RŪPA or MANO-RŪPA (mind-form). The mental body is also called the MĀYĀVI-RŪPA (illusory form), because in those dimensions everything is but thoughtforms which, though illusory, appear very real to the perceiver.

Mental Plane

The fifth of the seven great Planes of Being (counting from above). As the name implies, the Mental Plane is a world of *mind*. The lower four mental subplanes are the realm of the *concrete* mind or *rational* mind, which shapes mental matter into *thoughtforms*. The higher three subplanes (the Causal Worlds) are *formless* and correspond with the *Higher Mind* or *Abstract Mind*. The Human Soul (JĪVA) dwells on the formless levels of the Mental Plane. The seven subplanes of the Mental Plane are the true *Heaven Worlds*. DEVĀCHAN in Tibetan. SVARGA, SUVAH-LOKA and DEVASTHĀNA in Sanskrit.

Mind

From the Latin MENS, MENTIS. The word *mental* comes from the Latin MENTALIS. The ordinary human mind is *above* the physical body experience and *above* the astral, which is psychic and emotional, having to do with feelings. Your normal "thinking mind" is your mental body, which exists on the Mental Plane separately from your physical body. It is an organism *independent* of the physical body and brain. Thus, when you are not in the physical body, you can use your "mind" as a body in order to function independently in the Mental World. In the Esoteric Teachings, however, the word *mind* does not refer to just the little mind of a member of the human species, but the minds of angels, gods and demigods, as well as Cosmic Intelligences and the Great Cosmic Mind of the Creator-God Him/Herself.

Mokṣa

Sanskrit: Freedom, Liberation, Salvation. The Freedom of the Soul from birth and death in the lower worlds. The State of Everlasting Bliss above the Heaven Worlds. Also called Mukti (Liberation).

Monad

Greek: "The Indivisible One". The Whole, the All, the Complete, the One. The Greek word Monad means the same as the Latin Atom (primordial unit) and the ancient classical Sanskrit Aṇu. A Monad, Atom, Aṇu, can be the little world known by science as the "atom" or it can be a human being, a planet, a solar system or a galaxy; they are all atoms of various sizes. In relation to Humanity, the Monad is the Transcendental Spirit in Man, your "Father in Heaven", the I AM Presence in the innermost depths of the Soul (Paramātman, in Sanskrit). It is the God-Self, the highest point of Spirit within Man, dwelling on the Paranirvāṇic Plane.

Mystery Schools

The Mystery Schools were created in ancient Egypt, Greece and Rome to link up the lower to the higher, the visible to the invisible worlds. In the Mystery Schools one learnt about the invisible worlds surrounding us and penetrating us, and the meditational practices or Path by which one climbs up the worlds into the purely spiritual dimensions, Buddhi and Nirvāṇa, the Kingdom of God.

Nāda

Sanskrit: "The Soundless Sound". The Inner Sound. The Voice of the Silence. The Divine Word on the highest Spiritual Planes. The Pure Transcendental Sound of Absolute Reality. Nāda is the Word of the Spirit, the First Aspect of the Deity. It is the Originating-Sounding-Light-Vibration, the Source, Silence.

Name

The *Name* is the Power emanated from *within* God, from Universal Consciousness. The Greek Mystics and Mystery Schools called this Power the Logos (the Word). The ancient Persians called it Sraosha (the Word or Name-Power). In ancient India is was called Śabda (the Living Word or Sound-Current) and Nāma (the Name of God). It is invisible to physical eyes and permeates all of infinite Space and all the worlds, visible and invisible. The Name can be heard within the Heart as sweet Heavenly Music, and in the Head as the Cosmic-Ocean of Creative-Rumbling Word or Power, the Ocean-Tide of Life. Since very ancient times, the Mystics of all religions have called it by many Names, or expressions in human languages. These are known as the *Names of God* or *Divine Names*.

Nature

The word "Nature" does not just refer to what you behold with your physical eyes, for that is but an infinitesimal portion of the real Nature, the real Universe in which you "live, move and have your being". In Sanskrit, Nature is known as PRĀKṚTĪ, the matter or substance of all seven Planes of Being.

NIRMĀNAKĀYA

Sanskrit: The "Transformation Body" of a Buddha. A Buddha or Enlightened Being who remains in the Inner Worlds helping human evolution on all levels. These are the Saints, Yogīs and Masters of all religions who have attained Nirvāṇa but chose not to become absorbed in It (NIRVĀṆA-KĀYA). The NIRMĀNAKĀYAs are also known as BODHISATTVAs (those whose Essence is Love-Wisdom). Their Consciousness is focused in the Buddhic Plane, below Nirvāṇa. The NIRMĀNAKĀYAs have renounced Nirvāṇa in order to serve Humanity in the Inner Worlds, as far down as the Astral World. They are undying and Consciously Immortal, just like the NIRVĀṆĪs.

NIRVĀṆA

Sanskrit: Literally, "blown out, extinguished", from NIR (out, away from) and VĀṆA (to blow, to move). Commonly translated as "annihilation, destruction, dissolution". NIRVĀṆA is the blowing away of nescience, ignorance, darkness (MĀYĀ). NIRVĀṆA is Unconditioned Being, the annihilation of the personality in a Superior Consciousness, the cessation of Time, Space, form, matter and energy as we know them. In NIRVĀṆA one becomes One with the Universal "I AM", the Bright Self of the Universe.

ŌṀ

Sanskrit: The Word of Glory, the PRAṆAVA (Fundamental-Sound-Vibration of the Universe). ŌṀ is the Divine Word for Evolution, moving upwards and forwards and out of the Three Realms. ŌṀ is the Cosmic Word, the Logos, in the process of *ascending*, moving out of the Sphere of Creation-Activity. ŌṀ is the Sound of Purification and Union, Liberation and Resurrection, the Second Aspect of the Deity, the Christ Aspect or Power, the Sounding-Light Vibration which releases you from bondage to your forms and bodies. ŌṀ is the Formless-Self, the Sea of Pure Consciousness, Formless Awareness. ŌṀ is the Word of the Soul.

Omnipotent

From the Latin OMNI and POTENS: Infinite in power, unlimited in authority. All-powerful, mighty, supreme. A description of the Godhead.

Omnipresent

From the Latin OMNI and PRAESENS: Being present everywhere at the same time. Ubiquitous. A description of the Godhead. God is the all-enveloping Divine Law and Reality.

Omniscient

From the Latin OMNI and SCIENS: Having unlimited knowledge and understanding. The power to perceive and comprehend all things at once. A description of the Godhead.

PARABRAHMAN

Sanskrit: "Beyond Brahman". The Supreme Creative Intelligence. The One God. The Transcendental Reality. The Supreme Godhead. The Absolute Beingness. The Godhead beyond and above the Creator (BRAHMĀ). The Unknowable Absolute, which is limitless and which spreads Itself through endless Space. When in Creation, this Unmanifest Godhood forms a Veil upon Itself (MŪLAPRĀKṚTĪ) which conceals It from the sight of all created beings.

PARAMĀTMAN

Sanskrit: "The Supreme Being above the Universe." The Supreme Self, the Universal Self, the Eternal Self, the Transcendental Self, the Transcendental Spirit. The Universal Soul, the Over-Soul of the Universe. The Ancient of the Ancients, the Universal Godhead, the Light of Lights. The Absolute Being, the Absolute Existence, Universal Life. The MONAD, the "Father in Heaven". PARAMĀTMAN can be found and experienced in your Heart Centre. Within your Heart, the One Self, PARAMĀTMAN, can be seen. This One Self is within all forms, large or small, atomic or solar-systemic. When found in meditation, in deep Mystical Experience, PARAMĀTMAN will become your Inner Teacher and Guide, the SAT GURU.

PARANIRVĀṆA

Sanskrit: "Beyond Nirvāṇa". The Paranirvāṇic Plane is the realm of PARAMĀTMAN, the Monad, the "Father in Heaven", the Universal Divine Spirit in Man. Also called AṆUPĀDAKA (the Monadic World) and TAPAH-LOKA (the Fiery Realm).

Personality

The lower self. From the Latin PERSONA. In the old Roman days, a PERSONA was a mask an actor wore for a particular act or play. Thus, the personality is but a mask over the Soul. The Soul is immortal, the personality is not. At death the Soul gradually removes the personality or mask it has worn for that lifetime (the physical, etheric, astral and mental bodies). Personality means acting, pretending, role-playing, which people do so seriously!

Physical Plane

The seventh and last of the seven great Planes of Being. In Sanskrit, PṚTHIVĪ-LOKA or BHŪR-LOKA. The lower three subplanes of the Physical Plane are called the *dense* or *gross* physical subplanes, corresponding to the three states of matter that we observe with our physical senses: solids, liquids and gases. The higher four subplanes are called the *etheric* or *etheric-physical* dimensions. Science is beginning to explore the etheric dimensions, without understanding them as such.

Piscean Age

The zodiacal period of approximately 2,150 years, preceding the Aquarian Age. The Piscean Age is presently drawing to a close. The Stream of Energy that was predominant during the Piscean Age (the Sixth Ray) produced in Human Consciousness the phenomenon of intense *idealism*. The orientation of the Piscean Age was towards the Soul and the invisible worlds and Realities, towards "God" (howsoever people understood that word).

Planes of Being

The seven great Planes of Being are seven states of MAHAT-PRĀKṚTĪ (Cosmic Nature, the Cosmic Physical Plane). The Planes of Being are realms, worlds or conditions of existence. Each of the seven great Planes of Being, the seven dimensions of our Universe, occupies the one Space. The Space is the same, but the *dimensions* are different, the *densities of matter* are different, and the *consciousness* is different in each of the strata of Creation. The matter or substance of each plane *interpenetrates* the one below it, which is of lower vibration and greater density.

Planetary Logos

A "Heavenly Man" which incarnates through the vehicle of a planet. One of the Cosmic Creators.

PRĀṆA

Sanskrit: "Breath, Life-breath, Life-force, Vitality, Energy, Fire". PRĀṆA is the Universal Life-Force Fire, the Energy of the Universe which flows through all things. It is a spiritual and psychic Energy which becomes the five Elements and gives *substance* to all objects. PRĀṆA, the invisible Life-Force, permeates all the seven great planes of the Solar System from *within*. PRĀṆA is the Breath of Life, the Breath of God, the Universal Life-Force that energizes Creation.

PRĀṆĀYĀMA

Sanskrit: "Control of the Life-breath". From PRĀṆA (the Life-force, the Life-breath) and YĀMA (to regulate, to control, to guide). Conscious breathing. Regulation of the vital-force or PRĀṆA, the Breath of Life. PRĀṆĀYĀMA also means PRĀṆA-AYĀMA (no-control, spontaneous, natural). Thus, esoterically, PRĀṆĀYĀMA means breath which is natural, not forced, in balance, equilibrated. True PRĀṆĀYĀMA occurs when the in-breathing and the out-breathing are naturally suspended (transcended) and one attains the tranquil state of breath (PRĀṆAVĀYU), which produces the tranquil mind, SAMĀDHI. When your breathing is calm and steady, your mind is calm and steady. When your mind is calm and steady, your breathing is calm and steady.

PRATYEKA BUDDHA

Sanskrit: "An Enlightened One who walks alone". From BUDDHA (Enlightened One) and PRATYEKA (alone). A Solitary Buddha. A fully enlightened Buddha who, having attained Nirvāṇic Consciousness, merges into Nirvāṇa, never to return to the lower realms. The PRATYEKA BUDDHA has moved out of the human evolutionary field altogether and is therefore no longer accessible to Humanity on this planet.

PROPHETES

Greek: Someone who knows the Will of God, the *Plan*, through an interior revelation, by direct experience. One who speaks for God, the Deity. An inspired *revealer* or *interpreter* of the Divine Will, the Divine Plan. From the Greek PROPHECEIN, "to give religious instruction". From this came the English word *prophet*. A Prophet, in the Old Testament sense, and to the early Christians, was one who could speak on behalf of the Deity. Prophets were not confined to Israel only. Before Christianity, the Greeks and the ancient nations had many "prophets". The word, as used by them, had many distinct meanings.

Purgatory

The third, fourth and fifth subplanes of the Astral Plane, which appear to its denizens as very similar to the physical Earth. This is where ordinary people live after death. These people could be considered "earthbound" because their lives are a reflection of Physical Plane conditions and habits. For this reason these realms are sometimes called the *Reflection Sphere*.

Religion

From the Latin RE-LIGARE: "To tie, to fasten, to re-unite, to bind, to bring back". In the classical days of Rome, religion was an experience of Unity with the Divine, with the Godhead. Since the fourth century AD the word *religion* has been changed by the church to mean "a set of beliefs concerning the nature of the Universe and God; a set of fundamental (fundamentalist) beliefs and practices agreed upon by the church authorities; the practice of religious beliefs (dogmas), rituals and observances; faith, devotion, ritual, religious conviction".

Śabdabrahman (Śabda-Brahman)

Sanskrit: "The Sounding-God". The Sounding-Absolute. God Incarnate as the Eternal Word or Sound-Vibration. God as the Logos, Daiviprākṛtī, heard in deep meditation. The Incarnating Sound from which crystallizes the lower realms and worlds of Creation. All differentiations are caused by Śabda-Brahman. In each world, realm or region of the Universe, Śabda creates a different Vibration. Thus, on each plane of the Solar System, Śabda (Sounding-Light-Consciousness) arranges things differently. All forms, no matter how gross or subtle, are constructed by Sound-Vibration.

Sādhanā

Sanskrit: The Spiritual Life. Spiritual practice, spiritual discipline, quest. A Way or Path of Meditation consisting of the purification of the mind and the Heart, which results in the Union of the personal self with the Universal Self or Ātman.

Sādhu

Sanskrit: A good man, a virtuous man. A virtuous Saint who is a renunciate. A peculiarity of the sādhus and sannyāsins of India, and many yogīs, is their total lack of concern for their physical bodies and surroundings. This is caused by the shifting of the attention from personality-life into the Soul-life. Many of them exhibit abnormalities which Western psychology would classify as mental illness or psychotic behaviour. The aim of spiritual development, however, is to integrate or *synthesize* the human being so that he or she will become physical, imaginative, mental, intuitive and spiritual at the same time.

Saint

A true Saint is one who has attained Buddhic Consciousness or Nirvāṇic Consciousness. While a few of the Christian Saints were true Saints who entered the Kingdom of God, many were merely religious fanatics who converted people to the church, either by persuasion or by the sword. They were canonized by the popes because they converted people to the church, but they had no Higher Consciousness of any type. Furthermore, many *true* Saints were never recognized by the church. The church has always been totally confused about the true nature of a Saint.

Śakti

Sanskrit: "Energy, force, power, strength, might, ability, skill". The Divine Energy. God's Dynamic Energy. The Holy Spirit. Śakti is the Feminine side of the Deity. Śakti is the totality of the *real* Energy and Forces of this Universe, on all layers and levels, on all planes of Existence. She is the Goddess in all Her many forms, aspects and manifestations, and She is the Universal Mother, both as all forms and as the Life *within* forms. All the powers of the various Goddesses are but expressions of Śakti. All that Is is Energy (Śakti).

SAMĀDHI

Sanskrit: "The collecting together of the Intuitive or Direct Awareness of Reality", from SAMA (together) and DHĪ (the faculty of Intuition, the inner realizing principle). Equilibrated-mind (SAMĀ-DHI). The state of equilibrium, tranquil knowing, intuitive perception, passive awareness. That stage of DHYĀNA (meditation) wherein the mind is no longer disturbed by anything. The mystical trance-state, the suspended animation of your ordinary mind. The no-mind state wherein the ordinary mind of reason and logic does not function and you experience Causal Consciousness and Pure Consciousness.

SAṀSĀRA

Sanskrit: "Wandering" in the Three Worlds. Conditioned existence. Going around the Wheel of Birth and Death in the Three Worlds (the Physical, Astral and Mental Planes). SAṀSĀRA, our material Creation, essentially represents a realm of woe and unsatisfactory existence.

SAṀSKĀRA (SAṄSKĀRA)

Sanskrit: Previous subliminal (subconscious) impressions, or psychic imprints left over from previous embodiments. Mental behaviour resulting from past-life experiences and from previous experiences in this lifetime. Conditioning factors which give you your present moral and behavioural tendencies. Unconscious attachments to past habit patterns. The force of habits from the past. The karmic consequences of your past behavioural tendencies. SAṀSKĀRA are accumulations of latent impressions from the past which will work out now or in the future. From SAṀS (together) and KARA (acting, putting, doing). Impressions or grooves in the mental and astral bodies are "put together" from past thoughts, feelings and actions, which are the seeds for future Karma and Dharma. SAṀSKĀRA are produced by external circumstances, and by thoughts, feelings and physical actions, which form seeds for actions, propensities or impulses in this or future lifetimes.

SAMYAKSAṀ BUDDHA

Sanskrit: Perfectly-completely-Enlightened (SAMYAK-SAṀ-BUDDHA). A fully realized Buddha (above the ordinary Buddhas). A Buddha who has passed out of Human Evolution and who dwells in exalted conditions on the plane of MAHĀPARANIRVĀṆA.

SANAT KUMĀRA

Sanskrit: The Lord of the World, the Ancient of Days, the King of Kings, the Lord of Lords, the Master of Masters on this planet. SANAT KUMĀRA is the Undying Seed of Eternal Life, the Youth of Endless Summers, the Eternally Undying One.

Self-Realization

Realization of the Self (the Soul) and the SELF (the Spirit). In Sanskrit, ĀTMĀ-VIDYĀ, ĀTMĀ-JÑĀNA, ĀTMĀ-BODHA.

Seven Heavens

The seven subplanes (regions, vibratory states, dwelling places) of the Mental Plane, or DEVĀCHAN. These are the true Heavens, beyond the lower heavens of the Astral World.

Shaman

The word *shaman* is a degeneration of the original Sanskrit word ŚRAMANA (an ascetic training for spiritual powers). A shaman is a witch-doctor of the American Indians, the Eskimos, the Tibetans and the Mongolians. All are descendents of the old Atlanteans.

SHEKINAH

Hebrew: "Radiating Light, Glory as Light Emanation". The Divine Fiery Energy. God's Immanence. The Cloud of Glory or Brightness within Creation. The Glory of God's Presence, illuminating the world from within. The Glorious Hebrew Name SHEKINAH means the Light of NIRVĀṆA sent forth from the Infinite Light, AIN SOPH AUR. It is the Divine Presence in the Universe of Light, which is Feminine in nature towards the Boundless Godhead or Everlasting Light.

Solar Logos

A Cosmic Creator-God, such as our Sun. The physical body of our Solar Logos is our Solar System, and each planet is one of His cakras or "wheels of force". Many thousands of years ago these Creator-Gods (whose bodies are stars and planets) were called PRAJĀPATIs in India, DEMIURGOS and KOSMOKRATORES in old Greece, and ELOHĪM among the Semitic races of the Middle East.

Solar Plexus Centre

The Energy Centre which is responsible for your emotional well-being. All of your emotions, moods, feelings and desires go through it. It puts you in touch with the Astral World.

Spirit

The term *spirit* is often erroneously applied to disembodied beings on the Astral World, three planes below the realm of the true Human Spirit, ĀTMAN, the Self, dwelling on the Nirvāṇic Plane. The words *spirit* and *spiritual* come from the Latin SPIRITUS, which refers to both the Transcendent and Immanent aspects of God. The mediums degenerated the truth about *Spirit* and lowered it to astral phenomena.

Spiritual Hierarchy

Man's spiritual unfoldment is guided by the Planetary Hierarchy, the Great White Brotherhood, the Inner Government of the World, the Brotherhood of Light. It is also known as the Fifth Kingdom, the Kingdom of God, the Spiritual Kingdom, or the Christ-Hierarchy. It is the next human Hierarchy *above* the Human Hierarchy (the Fourth Kingdom). It is the Hierarchy of Saints, Masters, Yogīs and Teachers who have gone beyond the ordinary Man-type and are now evolving on the Causal, Buddhic and Nirvāṇic Planes. It is from these realms that the Hierarchy sends down AVATĀRAS, Divine Incarnations or Divine Messengers, to remind human beings of who they truly are, and to teach Mankind about the Kingdom of God. In Sanskrit, SAṄGHA or SATA-SAṄGHA.

Subconscious Mind

That which is *below* your conscious mind. The subjective mind, the dreaming mind, the symbolic mind. Dreamtime, imagination. The astral-body consciousness. In Sanskrit, SVAPNĀ-AVASTHĀ.

Subplane

Each of the seven great Planes of Being has seven subdivisions or *subplanes*—seven realms, spheres or vibrational states of increasingly finer matter or energy. Thus, there are a total of forty-nine subplanes, or states of matter, within the Cosmic Physical Plane of our Solar System. In the Secret Doctrine, the Primeval Wisdom, these forty-nine states of matter are called the *forty-nine Fires*.

SŪFĪ

Arabic-Persian: "One who has purified the Heart". One who has attained Mystical Union with God. A Pure One. A Muslim Saint. The SŪFĪs are all those great Saints of the Muslim religion who have attained Union with God, or who have merged into the Eternal Light. A SŪFĪ is "Pure in Heart" (QALB-SALĪM, a Heart that is Perfect). In the State of Perfection you perceive nothing else but God in all things, and the Divine becomes the Centre of your life, the Heart throb of your Being. Your personal ego is dissolved in God, FANĀ'FI-LLĀH.

ŚŪNYATĀ (ŚŪNYA)

Sanskrit: "Emptiness". A formless condition. A Buddhist term for the Mystical Consciousness (Buddhi), which is characterized by Formlessness, No-Thingness, Clarity, Light. NIRVĀṆA they call MAHĀŚŪNYATĀ (the Great Emptiness). To confuse the issue, some schools use this word to mean nonexistence or unreality. Others use this word to mean the sky or space.

TAO

Chinese: "The Great Absolute Ruler, the Heavenly-Master of Creation". TAO has been translated as "the One Truth or Reality underlying all Creation, the Single Principle of the Universe". Everything emerges out of TAO, develops and returns to its Source, which is TAO. TAO is the Essential Simplicity, which is the Source, Root and Origin of things, and at the same time, the Way, the Truth and the Life. It is the Manifest and Unmanifest Godhead all at once, in Oneness. TAO is the *Being* or *Essence* of all things, the *Source of Active Power* within all things, the *Force* or *Energy* behind all forms. Not originated by anything, it is the One Principle which is before all else. Thus, TAO cannot be talked about, but It can be *demonstrated* by Silence and Consciousness. Some people call TAO "God".

TAPAS, TAPASYA, TAPAḤ

Sanskrit: A burning longing for God or Liberation. Being on Fire for God and in God. Fiery Devotion, fiery effort in spiritual practice, the desire for Perfection, religious fervour, intense self-discipline, fiery aspiration, spiritual purification. Burning away impurities in the body, emotions and mind. Being on fire from the Fire within. TAPAS is the third NIYAMA (rule) of AṢṬĀṄGA YOGA, as set down by Patañjali. Scholars usually translate the word as "austerities". As practised by the common yogīs and ascetics, TAPAS came to mean "austerities, penance, harsh disciplines, punishing the physical body, self-torture", which have nothing at all to do with the original meaning. The word TAPAS literally means "being on fire" or "internal burning", from TĀPA (burning, fiery, heat, zealous). There is no suggestion in the word of torturing your body! TAPAS has to do with the Fire of the Mind; it can be translated as "self-discipline" or "mental discipline". It refers to disciplining one's thoughts, one's mental life, for the key to the Spiritual Path is mental regeneration, mind transformation. TAPAS has to do with interior purification of your whole Psyche or Inner Being by Inner Fire as you progress on the Spiritual Path through pure Devotion towards the Deity.

TAT

Sanskrit: "That". The Inconceivable Reality. The One Existence, the Final Truth, the Boundless Absolute, the Eternal Godhead. PARABRAHMAN (the Boundless All, the Absolute Godhead), PARABRAHM (the Infinite Invisible Existence). The final, inconceivable, indescribable Absolute Truth or Reality of the Godhead within Man and the Cosmos. The Spiritual Sun. The Unnameable.

THEOLOGIA

Greek: "God-Knowledge". The Science of God-Realization. From THEOS (God) and LOGOS (God as the Creative Principle, the Divine Word or Wisdom, the Divine Discourse or Reason). Hence the degenerated English word *theology*. In the early centuries of Christianity, theology was not just a set of intellectual ideas and dogmas as it is today. It was the *direct realization* of Divine Realities, the *inner perception* of the Spiritual Realms and Hierarchies through the processes of prayer, meditation and contemplation, the direct *realization* of God, deep within the Soul.

Third-Eye Centre

The Third-Eye is located between the eyes and is responsible for your ordinary mind, your mental body. It puts you in touch with the lower Mental Plane. When awakened, it becomes the seat of Spiritual Vision. It has been called the Wisdom-Eye, the Eye of Śiva, the All-Seeing Eye, the Single-Eye, the Spiritual Eye, the Clairvoyant Eye, and the Cyclopean Eye.

Thoughtform

A thought-structure existing in the mental body, built from matter of the lower mental subplanes. In Sanskrit, MANASI-JĀ, "things born from the mind". In your natural condition you are completely surrounded by your thoughtforms. Although you cannot see them with your physical eyes, your thoughts are objective, real, and you could see them if you had mental clairvoyance. These thoughtforms block your perception of Reality. When you drop your mental activity, you will come to know the Things that Are.

TORAH

Hebrew: "The Law". Religion, instruction. TORAH is popularly understood as the five Moses books of the Old Testament. (In the Jewish religion, the TORAH is a parchment scroll used in the synagogue, upon which is written the Law of Moses.) But in fact, TORAH is the Law of the Universal Mind, the Cosmic Mind, the Mind of God, the Mind of Light, which imposes its own Laws on every aspect, layer, condition or state of Creation. It is the Divine Order as it manifests throughout all Creation. There is also the Law (TORAH) as it applies to the species of Man. This has been the subject of the Teachings of all the great Teachers of Humanity. The Jewish idea of the TORAH teaches that Man is responsible for his Destiny or Fate. The *active* agent of the Law (KARMA) the Jews also know well as "the vengeance of the Lord", the retribution aspect of the Law, or Cause and Effect. The Hebrew word TORAH has the same significance as the Sanskrit word DHARMA. [See DHARMA and KARMA]

VĀSANĀ

Sanskrit: Desires for the future. Longings, unfulfilled hopes, desires, drives, urges and psychic impulses left over from previous lives. Subliminal imprints left over from the scars, seeds, pains, traumas, stresses or desires of previous lives, to be re-enacted in this life or future lives as subconscious drives. Habit-patterns acquired in previous existences which form the character of a child at birth, and which include all the subconscious cravings to which a man or woman is predisposed. [See SAṀSKĀRA]

Wisdom

Wisdom is called PRAJÑĀ or BODHI in Sanskrit, CHOCKMAH in Hebrew, SOPHIA in Greek, SAPIENTIA in Latin. In ancient times, these words did not mean being "worldly-wise", intellectual, or learned in our present sense, but the Knowledge that revealed the Path of Light. This is the mind-transcending, Truth-discerning Awareness of Pure Consciousness. It is pure Knowing, without words, without thoughts, without the mind.

YOGA

Sanskrit: "Joining together, yoking, aligning, linking, uniting, going into Oneness or Union". From YUGH, "to unite, join, put together, integrate". The State of Union. Union with the ĀTMAN. Union with God. YOGA also means "a method, an application of a principle, a means to an end, an arrangement, meditation, devotion". YOGA requires the control of the mind and the emotions. When the emotions and mind are tranquil, the breath (the Life-force, PRĀṆA) is harmonized and the Self (ĀTMA) is realized.

YOGA-NIDRĀ

Sanskrit: "The Sleep of the YOGĪ". This occurs when the Heart is awake and the rest of the human being is asleep. True YOGA-NIDRĀ is not falling off to sleep during meditation. In YOGA-NIDRĀ one's body and senses are at rest (asleep), while one's consciousness is wide awake inside.

YOGĪ, YOGIN, YOGINĪ

Sanskrit: "One who is united or integrated". A practitioner of the Science of Yoga (YOGA-MĀRGA). One who has attained the State of Union (YOGA), or SAMĀDHI. Or, one who has attained the highest state of Yoga or Union (Nirvāṇic Consciousness). A Saint of the Hindu and Esoteric Buddhist religions who has attained Union with ĀTMAN (the Universal Spirit) and BRAHMAN (the Ultimate Reality). A female YOGĪ or YOGIN is called a YOGINĪ.

SANSKRIT PRONUNCIATION GUIDE

~

VOWELS

A	AS IN F**A**THER
E	... TH**E**RE
I	... MACH**I**NE
O	... G**O**
U	... **FU**LL
Ṛ	... MER**RI**LY (ROLLED)
Ṝ	... MA**RI**NE
AI	... **AI**SLE
AU	... H**AU**S (GERMAN)

LONG VOWELS

Ā, Ī, Ū

THE LONG VOWELS ARE PRONOUNCED THE SAME AS THE SHORT VOWELS, BUT ARE OF LONGER DURATION (TWO OR THREE MEASURES). O AND E ARE ALWAYS SOUNDED LONG. THE LONG Ö INDICATES A PROLONGED SOUNDING.

SEMI-VOWELS

H	... **H**EAR
Y	... **Y**ET, LO**Y**AL
R	... **R**ED
V	... I**V**Y
	... MORE LIKE W WHEN FOLLOWING A CONSONANT
L	... **L**U**LL**

GUTTURAL CONSONANTS

SOUNDED IN THE THROAT.

K	... **K**EEP
KH	... IN**KH**ORN
G	... **G**ET, DO**G**
GH	... LO**GH**UT
Ṅ	... SI**NG** (NASAL)

PALATAL CONSONANTS

SOUNDED AT THE ROOF OF THE MOUTH.

C	... **CH**UR**CH**
CH	... **CH**AIN
J	... **J**UMP
JH	... HE**DG**EHOG
Ñ	... SE**Ñ**ORITA

CEREBRAL CONSONANTS

SOUNDED WITH THE TONGUE TURNED UP TO THE ROOF OF THE MOUTH.

Ṭ	... **T**RUE
ṬH	... AN**TH**ILL
Ḍ	... **D**RUM
ḌH	... RE**DH**AIRED
Ṇ	... **N**ONE

SANSKRIT PRONUNCIATION GUIDE

~

DENTAL CONSONANTS

SOUNDED WITH THE TIP OF THE TONGUE AT THE FRONT TEETH.

- T ... WA**T**ER
- TH ... NU**TH**OOK
- D ... **D**ICE
- DH ... A**DH**ERE
- N ... **N**OT

LABIAL CONSONANTS

SOUNDED AT THE LIPS.

- P ... **P**UT, SI**P**
- PH ... U**PH**ILL
- B ... **B**EAR
- BH ... A**BH**OR
- M ... **M**AP, JA**M**

SIBILANTS

THE SIBILANTS ARE HISSING SOUNDS.

- S ... **S**AINT
- Ś ... **S**URE
- Ṣ ... **SH**OULD, BU**SH**

NASAL SOUNDS

THE NASAL SOUNDS ARE SOUNDED AS A HUMMING IN THE ROOT OF NOSE. THE FOLLOWING REPRESENT INCREASING DEGREES OF NASALIZATION:

M, Ṁ, Ṅ (NG), ṄG

ASPIRATED SOUNDS

- H ASPIRATED OUT-BREATHING
- Ḥ DEEPER OUT-BREATHING

VARIATIONS

THE VOWELS Ṛ AND Ṝ ARE SOMETIMES WRITTEN AS ṚI, RI OR RĪ WHEN FALLING AT THE END OF A WORD.

FOR EXAMPLE: SĀVITRĪ

SOME COMMON EXAMPLES OF ANGLICIZED SPELLINGS

CAKRA	... 'CHAKRA'
ṚṢI	... 'RISHI'
SVĀMĪ	... 'SWAMI'
ŚAKTI	... 'SHAKTI'
ĀKĀŚA	... 'AKASHA'
KṚṢṆA	... 'KRISHNA'
ĀŚRAMA	... 'ASHRAM'
AVATĀRA	... 'AVATAR'

ANGLICIZED SPELLINGS APPEAR IN THIS WORK ONLY IN THE CONTEXT OF POPULAR USAGE.

ABOUT THE AUTHOR

~

Born in 1940 in Budapest, Hungary, Imre emigrated to New Zealand as a refugee at the age of sixteen. Since 1980 he has dedicated his life to teaching the Wisdom Science through his extensive writings and through workshops and retreats conducted around the world.

Imre's extraordinary knowledge of human spirituality is derived not from scholarly research, but issues forth from his own Interior Realization. He spans the full spectrum of human experience: reaching through time, illuminating the great Spiritual Teachings and Sacred Languages of our planetary history while pointing the way to the future. Imre's work is one of synthesis. His writing is universal, not biased towards any particular religion or tradition.

Imre Vallyon and Sounding-Light Publishing were awarded first place in the prestigious Ashton Wylie Charitable Trust Awards, and won a gold medal in the 2009 Living Now Awards, for the four-volume spiritual treatise *Heavens and Hells of the Mind.*

SELECTED TITLES

~

The New Planetary Reality
ISBN 978-0-909038-65-6

Planetary Transformation
ISBN 978-0-909038-61-8

Heavens & Hells of the Mind
ISBN 978-0-909038-30-4

The Magical Mind
ISBN 978-0-909038-11-8

The Warrior Code
ISBN 978-0-909038-64-9

The Sedona Talks
ISBN 978-0-9038-51-1

The Divine Plan
ISBN 978-0-909038-53-3

Heart to Heart Talks
ISBN 978-0-9038-55-4

The Art of Meditation
ISBN 978-0-9038-56-4

FOR MORE INFORMATION

~

Americas

PO Box 14227

San Francisco

CA 94114-0227

United States of America

Asia-Pacific

PO Box 771

Hamilton

New Zealand

Europe

PO Box 134

2000 AC Haarlem

The Netherlands

Online

www.planetary-transformation.org

www.soundinglight.com

info@soundinglight.com

CPSIA information can be obtained
at www.ICGtesting.com
Printed in the USA
FFOW05n1052250714

9 780909 038687